Most books on leadership and faith are either too abstract (boring and impractical) or too folksy (lightweight and self-absorbed). Roy's is neither. Instead, he deftly ties together hilarious misadventures, keen observations of human nature, and a close study of Scripture. The result is a book packed with memorable, practical leadership insights. No matter your job title, don't overlook the wisdom that comes from this junkyard entrepreneur–theologian. This is a rare book written by a rare individual.

JOSH KWAN, partner and cofounder of Praxis

Roy Goble is one of the finest leaders I know! He grew up in a junkyard, which taught him that even the unlikeliest characters can get the job done . . . often right under the noses of the powerful and privileged. That's what Roy sees in Scripture, too! Looking at the Bible through the lens of leadership—and vice versa—allows him to celebrate and cultivate the leadership ability of all people, regardless of their station in life. Although Roy is successful, he's also humble, which is reflected in this book's edgy sense of humor! This timely book is written from a grace-filled heart and years of practical experience. It's a fresh and effective addition to our necessary conversation about true leadership, and not just for those our culture assumes will lead. I highly recommend it!

BRENDA SALTER McNEIL, author of *Roadmap to Reconciliation: Moving Communities into Unity, Wholeness and Justice*

There are as many kinds of leaders as there are companies. What matters is not the style of a leader but rather the results. I know Roy to be a leader who drives the most essential sort of organizational growth: character. He may not know a thing about cloud technology, but I'd hire him tomorrow simply for his insights about people and purpose.

ANTONIO NERI, president and CEO of Hewlett Packard Enterprise

The scope of Roy's leadership journey is staggering. His stories will jar dormant parts of your brain into life, and his insights from those stories will have you thinking about leadership and following Jesus in new and refreshing ways. The pages of this book will make you laugh and drop your jaw, perhaps two of the most powerful ways to help us reimagine.

NANCY ORTBERG, CEO of Transforming the Bay with Christ

Entertaining, easy to read, down-to-earth, and authentic. The levity and stories of an era I remember all too well brought transparency and made for good reflection. The deep leadership takeaways were there in a vernacular that made them thought-provoking.

AL MIYASHITA, NYC city director of The Navigators

Salvaged is the common-sense leadership guide you've been waiting for. I say "guide" because Roy doesn't insist on one-size-fits-all conclusions. Rather, he explores the terrain of everyday leadership, from the junkyard all the way to the boardroom, and invites his readers along on the journey. By turns self-effacing, serious, and humorous, Roy encourages readers to ask better questions, to demand better answers, and most of all to laugh at themselves. No matter their occupation, readers will find the practical wisdom they need to take their leadership ability to the next level.

MARK ZORADI, CEO of Cinemark Holdings and former president of Walt Disney Motion Picture Group

"This book sucks" . . . is something I've never said after reading one of Roy's books. Not your typical regurgitated tome on leadership, *Salvaged* plunges deep into the reality of working with people—it's a messy business, regardless of whether it happens in the boardroom or in the junkyard. With his trademark humor on full display, Roy uncovers deep truths about real-world, biblical leadership while also delivering a genuinely FUN read. His colorful characters and lighthearted parables are as memorable as they are entertaining—these are lessons that will actually stick!

JON BEEKMAN, CEO of Man Crates

I've read very few books on leadership that help me in the unique and nuanced situations that arise each day, but *Salvaged* does exactly that. Roy Goble, like me, had a father who greatly influenced his leadership style. Now Roy looks back with the eye of a master storyteller, distilling his varied experiences into relevant lessons we all need. Being a results-driven, Jesus-following businessperson is not for wimps—but Jesus wasn't a wimp either!

JODY VANDERWEL, managing partner of Grand Angels Venture Fund II

Salvaged is the leadership book I have been waiting for. Through the power of story, Roy uses humor, honesty, and the cold hard truth about teams, self-awareness, and working with people. This is a journey through life lessons and the wisdom that comes from turning wounds into the evidence of healing. The authenticity displayed by Roy makes you want to sit down with him to hear even more. You will be captivated by the examples and stories while thinking, *I can't believe he just said that*. *Salvaged* is a refreshing read on leadership that lets you know you're not alone and that even in the junkyard, you can turn a mess into a miracle. This is more than a leadership book; it's a redeeming therapy session for anyone looking for a new way forward in the workplace and in life.

ROMAL TUNE, author of *Love Is an Inside Job: Getting Vulnerable with God*

Goble wrote a *book*?

RICH, junkyard coworker from back in the day

SALVAGED

LEADERSHIP LESSONS PULLED FROM THE JUNKYARD

ROY GOBLE

WITH D. R. JACOBSEN

NavPress is the publishing ministry of The Navigators, an international Christian organization and leader in personal spiritual development. NavPress is committed to helping people grow spiritually and enjoy lives of meaning and hope through personal and group resources that are biblically rooted, culturally relevant, and highly practical.

For more information, visit www.NavPress.com.

Salvaged: Leadership Lessons Pulled from the Junkyard

Copyright © 2018 by Roy Goble. All rights reserved.

A NavPress resource published in alliance with Tyndale House Publishers, Inc.

NAVPRESS is a registered trademark of NavPress, The Navigators, Colorado Springs, CO. The NAVPRESS logo is a trademark of NavPress, The Navigators. *TYNDALE* is a registered trademark of Tyndale House Publishers, Inc. Absence of ® in connection with marks of NavPress or other parties does not indicate an absence of registration of those marks.

The Team:
Don Pape, Publisher
David Zimmerman, Acquisitions Editor
Elizabeth Symm, Copy Editor
Dean H. Renninger, Designer

Cover photograph of gears copyright © by YagiStudio/Getty Images. All rights reserved.

Author photograph provided by author; used with permission.

Published in association with literary agent Tawny Johnson of D. C. Jacobson & Associates LLC, an Author Management Company, www.dcjacobson.com.

For information about special discounts for bulk purchases, please contact Tyndale House Publishers at csresponse@tyndale.com, or call 1-800-323-9400.

Cataloging-in-Publication Data is available.

ISBN 978-1-63146-956-5

Printed in the United States of America

24   23   22   21   20   19   18
7   6   5   4   3   2   1

For my father, Ernie Goble, who always modeled
his own unique style of leadership.

Acta Non Verba

CONTENTS

SECTION THREE

SECTION FOUR

FOREWORD

Roy Goble is my first friend.

We met in Mrs. Martini's first-grade classroom in San Jose, California. Probably standing in line, which we did a lot. Goble came just before Goff, so we had plenty of time to get to know each other. He was a guy who was always getting into the good kind of mischief, and I was drawn to him like a magnet.

I didn't have the words to tell Roy at the time, but that was a tough age for me. Even that young, I felt like an outsider. Standing taller than nearly all of my classmates made it hard to hide. Feeling shy made it hard to find friends.

Roy was the one who brought me into his circle of buddies. That meant getting invited to sleepovers, sharing food out of our lunch boxes, and doing lots of laughing. It meant never being alone on the playground. It meant discovering love and acceptance.

Which meant the world to an awkward kid like me.

The best thing about Roy's friendship was that he chose

me, on his own, because he figured it would be fun. He already had plenty of friends. No one told him to be nice to the new kid or anything like that. But Roy assumed life would be better together.

This book on leadership is more of the same from Roy. It's fun, mischievous, and welcoming. A little edgy, too, but it always values love and Jesus as essential to leadership.

Roy's been leading since we were kids. He was the one who organized sleepovers and captained our basketball and football games on the playground. He'd be one of the first to stand up for his friends and one of the first to laugh at himself when he messed up.

Not that life was all soda and bubble gum with Roy. Our group shot marbles as often as we could and occasionally played winner takes all. Roy and I were pretty good, but one time we got wiped out by older kids whose extra-large marbles made it easy for them to beat us. After the second or third time we'd lost our marbles,[1] Roy decided to change the equation. The next day he showed up with extra-large marbles made of solid steel. The older kids raised a stink, but the marbles were round and Roy insisted on playing with them. We mopped the floor with the older kids, and it was only later that I learned we'd been playing with industrial ball bearings Roy had snagged from his dad's junkyard!

The year we turned eleven was the year every kid we knew wanted to look like Keith Partridge, including me. With my

---

[1] Now that we're nearing sixty, we've lost our marbles many, *many* more times.

red hair and freckles, I looked more like Danny Partridge, but at least he was still in the band. It would take some time to grow out feathered bangs and a wavy mullet, so I figured I'd start by getting my mom to buy me a shirt with an outrageously wide butterfly collar, plus some bell-bottoms and a matching vest.

Roy shrugged and continued to wear his Levi's blue jeans and short-sleeve button-down shirts. When I asked him why he wasn't getting on the Partridge bus with the rest of us, he told me all those fancy clothes made people look silly. And then he asked why I wanted to let some Hollywood know-nothing tell me how to dress, and also why *I* wanted to look silly!

Great questions.

That was fifty-some years ago, and Roy still jokes with me and pushes me to be a better person. And that's probably what makes him a great leader: He pushes people to be their best but never makes them feel bad. I wish we'd spent even more time together as kids. Who knows what cool stuff I might have learned along the way. I'm still a little jealous I wasn't hanging out with him that day in the junkyard when he built his homemade bazooka.

Here's where I could pivot to some amazing example of Roy's leadership as an adult, from Silicon Valley to the rain forests of Belize. But I won't. I want to focus on our distant past because it speaks so powerfully about today.

My first friend pointed me in the right direction. When Roy took a chance on me, it helped *me* take a chance on me.

It helped me become me. And that's exactly what I've watched him do for others, ever since we conquered the marble mafia at Booksin Elementary.

I guess what I'm saying is that nothing Roy does as a grown-up surprises me, in a good way, because I've known him for so long. I expect Roy to do Kingdom business, I expect him to lead counterintuitively and faithfully, I expect him to welcome new friends and new voices, and he does.

See, back when the rest of us kids were still trying to figure it all out, Roy was already leading. Not that he had it all figured out either. He just refused to let a lack of certainty stop him!

Roy lives the same way today. Leadership is built into his character, and he's never tuned it out or turned it off.

But I still won't play marbles with him.

Bob Goff
San Diego, California

INTRODUCTION
WHY ANOTHER CRAPPY LEADERSHIP BOOK?

The *only* people who should write leadership books are the ones who have failed while attempting to follow Jesus in the workplace.

I'm one of those folks, as you'll soon discover.

I've failed six ways from Sunday. I tell quite a few of those stories in this book and quite a few others in my first book.[1] And I've been leading, in one form or another, every day of my adult life.

I bet you have too. Led every day, that is—not failed every day. We're all leaders, whether or not we're used to thinking about it that way.

In my case I am, or have been, a business owner, an involved church member, an employee,[2] a board member, a parent, and a nonprofit leader. It doesn't matter if I'm having a bad day or don't feel up to setting an example or serving . . . I'm still leading.

---

[1] I haven't used *all* my stories, of course—gotta save some for future use!
[2] Employees are leaders too.

And you? Well, if you're reading this, you might lead a team of employees in an air-conditioned office, work with a crew on a construction site or as a nurse in a hospital, or file paperwork from home in your pajamas. Maybe you're a single parent, a Little League coach, or a food-pantry volunteer. Perhaps you sing with your church's worship team, deliver mail, drive a tow truck, wash dishes at a restaurant, sell insurance, or sit in a coffee shop writing all day.[3]

At some point in your daily routine, do you make decisions that impact others? Like figuring out how to fix the office copier or deciding how much salt to add to the guacamole dip for your guests? If so, then you are able to "define reality," as Max De Pree famously said.[4] You're a leader.

Living is leading. Leadership doesn't belong only to those with a platform or a high-profile job. If you're alive, you're leading.

See, despite the gurus who want to privatize and monopolize leadership, we all lead in some capacity. Even MBA types occasionally manage to lead! Teachers lead classrooms. Small-business owners lead employees, vendors, and customers. The UPS driver is leading every time she responds to a customer upset about a late package, and the carpenter on a construction site leads every time he responds to a change order. All of us make decisions that impact people every day, sometimes on the fly without all the information we need. Each time we do this, we're

---

[3] Or worse, sit in an office editing the things a guy in a coffee shop writes all day.
[4] Max De Pree, *Leadership Is an Art* (New York: Doubleday, 1989).

leading because we are drawing people toward our vision of what needs to happen.

Just as I lead every day, I try to follow Jesus every day . . . and I'm liable to fail at either, or both.

That tension is the reason you're reading this book. For most people, leading is a *default*, but obeying Jesus is a *choice*. Following Jesus seven days a week takes effort and intentionality. We need to be active, wise, and consistent. We have to be willing to take risks, which means being willing to fail.

And how can a "failure" be a leader, let alone a leadership guru who writes leadership books?

After all, most leaders give the impression of perfection. Even their occasional admissions of failure are carefully chosen to present them in a safe, reputable light. However, the reality of leadership—and the Christian life—is far messier! Leaders who pen books about greatness are not always great. Yet the leadership books march irresistibly forward, to the tune of more than fifty thousand and counting on a recent Amazon search.

With that many voices, how can we know who we should listen to?

For starters, we shouldn't listen to books that aim over the heads of most actual, day-to-day leaders. Neither should we listen when formulaic solutions are applied to nuanced, complicated problems.[5] And we shouldn't pay attention to answers so spiritualized and sanitized that they aren't relevant to the messy reality of following Jesus.

---

[5] In this book, you might find the occasional sentence that sounds like a formula. The difference is that I'll contradict it a few pages later—and usually on purpose!

Most of us need a different perspective on leadership. My aim is to leverage my background—from junkyards to cattle ranches, from real estate companies to nonprofit boards, from global missions to local churches, from small-scale failures to larger-scale stupidity, from loving husband and father to successful business investor—in order to offer a more pragmatic approach to leadership.

Hopefully, this is a more *effective* approach. Most of us aren't going to start the "next big thing" tomorrow, but we will need to solve problems, balance truth with compassion, and—as my junkyard friends would say a bit more colorfully—get stuff done.

In that spirit, let me tell you a bit about who I am by way of who I'm not.

I'm not an academic.

I'm not a megachurch pastor.

I'm not a Harvard Business School graduate.

I don't work in a corner office or have personal assistants to do everything for me.[6]

The interior of my car sports a combination of dog hair, hay, and mud. I don't get what little is left of my hair cut by some overpriced stylist, and I certainly don't wear fancy suits to work. In fact, my typical work attire includes boots (that's how the mud gets into my car) and jeans (which I sometimes buy used on eBay).

What I *am* is a follower of Jesus who goes to work every day. Since I fail, I want to do better.

---

[6] My assistant Anne gets as much done as ten PAs, anyway.

Sound familiar?

I do recognize the greatness of particular leaders, of course, and I learn from them. A few even write great books. Not all the leadership information available is narcissistic or indecipherably academic. But there *is* usually something missing.

Unfortunately, what's missing is *not* a magic formula or simple method! It would be amazing if I had a memorable acronym or a TED-level Thought Leader Insight.[7] But I don't. All I've got is a willingness to wrestle.[8] Tensions are *everywhere* when you're a follower of Jesus and a leader. It's tempting to look for formulas or quick fixes, but that's not what we signed up for when we said *yes* to Jesus. Ours must be "a long obedience in the same direction,"[9] a series of daily decisions we must make over and over and over. Leading well can be a slog. It can be frustrating and murky. There will be good days and bad days . . . and bad weeks and years. If we're not certain *why* we're taking the long way around, we'll inevitably settle for a shortcut.

I'm tired of the truth being sugarcoated. I'm sick of BS[10] about how "easy" or "simple" it is to follow Jesus while working. If we want to succeed at following Jesus *and* leading—and be the same person seven days a week—we need to pursue the *full* truth, not tweet-friendly platitudes.

---

[7] If you are in charge of booking TED Talks, though, give me a call. I'm sure I can invent some convincing jargon after a few glasses of wine.

[8] My first book, *Junkyard Wisdom: Resisting the Whisper of Wealth in a World of Broken Parts* (Sisters, OR: Deep River Books, 2016), is about wrestling with the tension of wealth and discipleship.

[9] Eugene H. Peterson, *A Long Obedience in the Same Direction*, 2nd ed. (Downers Grove, IL: InterVarsity, 2000).

[10] Biblical scholarship, obviously.

So, what do I hope you get out of this book?

A willingness to step into the contradictions and messiness of leadership, first and foremost. You might even find times when I contradict myself in this book, or maybe I'm not entirely clear about something. Well, that's in part by design. Just like Scripture, just like the teachings of Jesus, not much in life is linear. The same is true for leadership.

Second, I hope you find yourself laughing at times. I think best about myself, and others, when I'm laughing. There is a clarity that comes in those moments when we relax, let down our guard, and simply laugh out loud at the silliness of it all—and God laughs with us in those moments. (And quite likely *at* us, as a father laughs at his child doing funny things.) So quite a few chapters contain stories or insights that I hope will make you laugh at the sheer audacity of attempting to lead well while following Jesus faithfully. Leading well and following Jesus is not a laughing matter, obviously. But it will generate a lot of stories . . . and some of them might end up with poisoned rats raining down from the rafters.

Most leaders don't pursue Jesus. Many followers of Jesus don't pursue effective, results-based leadership. The following thirty-one stories are about what happens at the intersection of your job and following Jesus. We're going to explore how real people can lead by answering God's call on their lives.

We're also going to talk about homemade bazookas, because they're awesome.

If we can't laugh at life—and especially at ourselves—we can never hope to lead well. And when we're done laughing, perhaps we'll discover an expanded understanding of how following Jesus on a daily basis can transform us, over time, into leaders of substance and consequence, no matter our occupation.

Third, I hope you get to know some of the amazing characters who have changed my life for the better.

Especially my father. He looms large in this book and in my heart. Dad was a larger-than-life, self-made man who went from dirt-poor Okie to junkyard operator to Silicon Valley real estate success story. He was John Wayne without the tendency toward drink or fistfights and a faithful member of the same Baptist church for more than fifty years. He had an intuitive business sense that included everything from pool halls to wrecking yards to steam cleaners to coin-operated car washes to pig farms.[11] Some worked, some didn't, but he was willing to try almost anything. His pig farm was especially funny: He found a bakery that gave away all their day-old food, so he tried to raise pigs on nothing but Twinkies and expired Wonder Bread. It didn't work out so well.

Dad loved three things passionately: God, his family, and business. He wanted to combine family and business at every opportunity, in part because he could do what he loved with the people he loved. He adored his grandkids, making them laugh about "training" his car to pull into every donut shop they passed.[12] Dad sang every song, even "Amazing Grace,"

---

[11] And I do mean intuitive. He never had a class on accounting or business management or any sort of business training. His "strategic plan" was usually a few calculations on the back of a napkin.

[12] He'd throw his hands up and use his knees to steer the car into the donut shop parking lot. Not exactly safe and sane driving, especially when his grandkids had to continually remind him to put on a seat belt and watch where he was going, but memorable nonetheless.

with the lyrics from "Home on the Range," thought nothing of twelve-hour workdays six days a week, and was happily dealing with rambunctious cattle at the age of eighty.[13] Tired of always losing socks and having to throw a single one away, he headed to Macy's and bought two hundred pairs of the exact same style so they'd all match. He "stole" so many pens from my desk I finally gave him one thousand ballpoint pens for his birthday, and it only took him three months to lose them all. Dad was a tolerant, gentle man who had little use for laziness or naysayers, and he lived his life by the motto *Acta Non Verba*, "deeds not words." Nobody ever controlled my fiercely independent father. If he saw a sign telling him not to walk on the grass, he'd pack a picnic and sit right down. And those of us who had the honor of living alongside him were better for it.

Another character is my dad's junkyard, the place where I practically grew up. Like my dad, the junkyard was *quite* a character. It's where I learned to work and where I learned to lead. Out back was an open field, soaked with grease and crammed with dusty cars, usually in random order, valued more for their parts than their whole. Life is a bit like that too, both for better and for worse. It's messy and dirty, but all too often we try to sterilize things. Sometimes sterilization is good . . . but sometimes it removes the very grease that keeps the wheels moving forward. Finding that balance isn't easy,

---

[13] Until a bull decided to charge him. Dad was run over and broke his neck. Didn't stop him from living, though, as a few months later he loaded up a limo with his high-school buddies and they retraced Highway 66 back to their roots in Oklahoma.

but learning a bit about my friend the junkyard might shed a little light on things for you.

Finally, I hope you get to know me a bit. I grew up in a middle-class suburban neighborhood, worked at my dad's junkyard on Saturdays, and attended a large and dynamic church on Sundays. When I was in middle school, we moved to a cattle ranch, where I learned to ride and brand, and then I moved to the beauty of Santa Barbara for college. Just after graduation, I married D'Aun, joined my dad's growing real estate business, and began doing deals in what we now call Silicon Valley. This often meant overseeing construction crews and management teams while negotiating with contractors and agents. D'Aun and I started the first ever faith-based environmental organization when we were in our twenties, which led us to the High Sierra, the plains of Zimbabwe, and Central American rainforests. Somewhere along the way, we helped plant a church, raised two great kids, remodeled or built a half dozen homes, started an olive oil business, managed a vineyard, and launched an education ministry for at-risk youth.

Throughout it all, I was leading in some way, shape, or form. Even when I was the kid in the junkyard, or herding cattle into a pen, or sipping coffee at a hip spot in Haight-Ashbury while mentoring a future leader, or simply sitting in my backyard with a glass of wine and a few friends talking about theology, I was leading.

And undoubtedly you have similar stories to tell, or will

have by the time you're my age. Because as I said, we're all leaders.

Too often we think *others* are the leaders who matter. And too often we think improving leadership means massive changes and paradigm shifts.

Truth is, *we* are the leaders who matter, and we can improve the way we lead, beginning now.[14]

---

14 Not *right* now, because you're probably using the "Look Inside" feature online. Buy it, read another chapter or two, and then start applying what I say . . . or at least avoiding the mistakes I've made.

SECTION ONE

WITH ALL DUE RESPECT
TO ROBERT FULGHUM, ALL I REALLY
NEEDED TO KNOW ABOUT LEADERSHIP
I LEARNED IN THE JUNKYARD.

1
CAKE AND PICKLES (AND NO, I'M NOT PREGNANT)

We need to know what motivates us—and those around us— if we're going to lead well.

"Have you tried the fried scorpion on a bed of jackfruit?"

I'd been eyeing the scorpion, but now I looked up to see a smiling young woman encouraging me to try this strange concoction. My wife, D'Aun, and I were attending the annual Explorers Club banquet in New York, all dressed up in a traditional gown and tux . . . but the appetizers on offer were, well, *weird*. Not just scorpions, but boiled tarantulas, jellyfish salad, and baked iguana.

Okay, I thought, *there's a time for everything*. I lifted the scorpion by the toothpick protruding from its back and then gulped it down. And you know what? It wasn't bad at all!

I doubt I'll start scarfing down scorpions whenever I get

the chance. I just turned sixty, and adding arachnids to my diet isn't one of my goals. But the experience reminded me of something: the weird food cravings many of us experience. A friend of mine can't watch a movie without buttered popcorn and a glass of Chardonnay. Other friends swear by strawberries covered in balsamic vinegar. Some put sugar on tomatoes and salt on watermelon. And my late father . . . well, he was in a category all his own.

My father was a child of the Great Depression. Although he was born in Montana, his mother passed away when he was young, and his father moved the family to Oklahoma . . . just in time for a little thing called The Dust Bowl. Like so many others, they headed west, looking for all the world like characters from Steinbeck's *The Grapes of Wrath*. When they arrived in Northern California, they tried to put down roots,[1] but life remained tough.

It wasn't unusual for Dad to go a whole day without food. But like a lot of folks in that era, Dad was resilient and creative at finding what he needed to get by.

For instance, in the small town of Port Chicago where they lived, churches and community groups would throw the occasional party. Dad kept an ear to the ground, and when he heard about a potluck dinner he'd simply wander into whatever lodge or church fellowship hall was hosting the event. With all the attendees milling around the buffet tables, scarcely anyone noticed a small boy—and if they did, most kindly looked the other way. Folks knew others were hungry.

---

[1] A task made easier by the fact that their home was a tent with a mud floor.

Imagine a rail-thin boy staring at long tables covered in a cornucopia of church-lady foods. Tuna hotdish. Potato cakes. Bowls filled with mints and mixed nuts. Jars of pickles. Biscuits. Bean-and-sausage casserole. Corn. Pound cake. Sheet cake. Lemonade and coffee.

Now imagine that boy having the good grace (and sense) not to barge to the front of the line, and instead hanging back and filling his plate with leftovers. It may have been a function of the culinary tastes in that particular neck of the woods, but there were nearly always leftover chocolate cake and pickles. Cake, of course, because there are always *way* too many desserts at buffets, and pickles, because most people who toss a pickle on their plate don't actually *eat* the pickle. Dad, however, happily gorged himself on that unlikely combination. The bizarre result of Dad's forays into the buffet lines of Port Chicago was an unexpected—and long-lasting—fancy for that stomach-turning mix of sugar and vinegar.

In fact, my father carried that penchant through the rest of his days. Even when he could buy any food he wanted, he continued to eat the occasional plate of chocolate cake and pickles. He never made a big deal of it, and in some ways, it embarrassed him, especially as he became more successful. Eating that strange mixture brought him back to his roots, however. It reminded him of his humble beginnings and the excitement he felt on those days when he discovered a surplus of calories.

We're all like my father in some ways. We each have

cravings. For some of us, it's food, and for others, it's praise. We might be experience junkies or adrenaline chasers. An ever-increasing paycheck motivates some while others are always on the lookout for more friends.

Our cravings can be exploited if we're not careful. When I was younger, I'd offer my dad chocolate cake and pickles when I wanted him to do me a favor! He never actually fell for it, but he always laughed, and I think he admired my attempt. Wise leaders must be familiar with both their own motivations and what motivates their teams . . . and then use that knowledge for good rather than exploitation.

SALVAGED FROM SCRIPTURE

Scripture is full of characters with cravings. Some cravings motivated behavior that was reprehensible. Consider David, who craved Bathsheba enough to commit murder. At least once, craving produced some good old-fashioned stupid when Esau traded his inheritance for a single bowl of stew. We are all tempted to give in to these unhealthy cravings.

But there are also examples when cravings were expressed in positive, healthy ways.

The Psalms are filled with cravings for the presence of God.[2] The Proverbs express passion for God's Word over and over. Nehemiah was motivated by God's glory. The apostle Paul seemed driven by his deep compassion for those in the Roman world who had not heard the gospel. Esther had a

---

[2] Strangely, many of those psalms were written by a man who craved adultery and committed murder. The Bible, like life, refuses to be neat and tidy.

deep sense of responsibility to her people, combined with a courage only a woman of faith could muster. Likewise, Ruth was motivated by a deep faith and sense of responsibility for her family commitments.

All of these characters were motivated by healthy passions to honor God through their work.

Getting our cravings in line is going to make us stronger leaders. And understanding the motivations (the cravings) of our teams will allow us to set appropriate incentives. We're not all going to be like Paul or Esther or Ruth. But we're not all going to be Esau either. And understanding these motivations will allow us to properly channel our instincts toward healthy goals.

LESSONS FROM THE JUNKYARD

Our cravings can be exploited if we're not careful.

Getting our cravings in line is going to make us stronger leaders.

Understanding the motivations of our teams will allow us to set appropriate incentives.

2
AIM HIGH! (ESPECIALLY WITH AN ACETYLENE-POWERED HOMEMADE BAZOOKA)

We rarely achieve 100 percent of what we attempt—which is why we should attempt more than we hope to achieve.

Caution: This chapter has the feel of one of those motivational posters you see on the walls of middle-management offices. But unlike those posters, I think you'll find this chapter amusing.

One unmotivated summer afternoon in the junkyard, I turned to a pastime common to young boys: I began to think about bazookas.

It so happened that the guy I was supposed to be working with was *also* thinking about bazookas. I can't remember his name, but he was young and foolish, so naturally I loved hanging out with him. For the purposes of this story, I'll give him an innocent pseudonym. Hmm . . . okay, got one.

So Bozo and I had heard through the grapevine that you could take the driveline out of a car and repurpose it as a bazooka.[1] That afternoon, after concluding (in our wisdom) that the information sounded solid, we shirked our work and instead found an old driveline that was about five feet long.

From there, our process was simple. At a roughly forty-five-degree angle, Bozo welded the driveline to the yard truck.[2] Next, we crammed some old rags about halfway down, followed by a greasy tennis ball that one of the dogs had rejected.

"This thing's gonna launch into the next time zone!" crowed Bozo, though his language was more colorful and less aware of things like time zones. I nodded eagerly.

All that remained was propellant, and since it was our first time with a homemade bazooka, we decided to use the most flammable thing we could get our hands on: acetylene. It fueled the cutting torches used to pull apart cars.

We removed ourselves to a safe distance—six feet was plenty!—and began to flick lit matches at the bottom of the driveline. The third one ignited the acetylene, producing a sound that can best be described as . . . how can I put this . . . *WWWHHHOOOMMMPPPHHH!* The tennis ball exited our makeshift bazooka at an unholy velocity, shooting up and up and up . . .

---

[1] To get a bit technical on you, the driveline is the tube-thingy that connects the power from the front-mounted engine to the rear wheels. This was back in the day when they were long, wide, and hollow (today they tend to be short and solid). Cut off the ends, and you're left with a remarkably strong tube.

[2] Yard trucks were part pickup, part tow truck, unregistered, usually without any glass, sometimes without doors. We used them to move cars and parts around.

. . . for about 0.02 seconds. That's when it smacked directly into the side of the sheet-metal shop building, producing a decibel level somewhere between a jet taking off and a nuclear bomb.

Luckily, the only people inside the shop at that time were most of our employees and all of our customers. And my dad.

I had a moment to reflect. On the plus side, I'd fired a homemade bazooka, and how many kids could say that? On the minus side, my life was about to end.

Dad boiled out of the shop like an angry hornet, and he sure *looked* like he wanted to kill me! Once he sized up the situation, however, he chose the way of mercy—as he so often did—and allowed me to live. Dad docked my pay and assigned me to some of the nastiest cleanup work he could find, which definitely included close proximity to (a) rodents and (b) toxic chemicals.[3]

Bozo and I did learn our lesson; I'll give Dad credit for that. Never again did we use potentially deadly, highly flammable acetylene to launch a tennis ball at high speed from a jerry-rigged bazooka into the side of our shop building.

Nope.

Next time, after rewelding the bazooka and adjusting our aim, we cleared the shop by a good twenty feet. We also cleared the street outside and half the industrial park across the street. So we did it again. And again. I've always wondered what those folks thought when tennis balls started dropping from the sky!

---

[3] Those were the good ol' days!

SALVAGED FROM SCRIPTURE

You know who literally aimed high? David the giant killer.

David and Goliath is one of the top five Sunday-school stories, and kids hear it pretty early, even though it ends with a decapitation.[4] We often teach that story as a lesson about the underdog pulling off an unlikely win, but what if David was actually *favored* in the fight? (Note: I recommend you read Malcolm Gladwell's take on the David and Goliath story, found in *David and Goliath: Underdogs, Misfits, and the Art of Battling Giants*. It's a great read, and I'm borrowing some of his ideas here.)

Picture a six-foot-five-inch infantry grunt in full body armor lugging a Kevlar shield. He's ready to kick in some doors and some teeth! Fearsome, sure, but not to everyone— and certainly not to the five-foot-four-inch sniper who's prone on a rooftop down the street. David was wielding what amounted to the sniper rifle of his day, and Goliath—with his bad eyesight, cumbersome equipment, and slow-moving body—was a sitting duck. David didn't win as some plucky underdog. Rather, he leveraged his wiry shepherd muscles, quick reflexes, and superior technology—and yes, God's Spirit—to take down a giant.

Perhaps we've learned the wrong lesson from the David and Goliath story. Or rather, a *lesser* lesson. Have you ever achieved 100 percent of what you attempted as a leader?

---

[4] Decapitation isn't the worst in the Old Testament, either. We could also make Sunday-school lessons about . . . let's see . . . Jael using a hammer to drive a tent peg through a guy's temple (Judges 4:21), Ehud driving his short sword so deeply into a fat king's abdomen that the hilt disappears (Judges 3:21-22), or how about the ground opening up and swallowing a bunch of families (Numbers 16:28-33)? Fun!

Your failure to do that doesn't mean you should attempt less, however—it means you should attempt more![5]

Like the motivational posters say, think smart, come prepared, aim high, and don't be intimidated. Bozo and I had the second part of that advice down pat. Effective leaders do the whole thing. The next time you face down a challenge, you might be favored, rather than the underdog. So aim high. What do you have to lose?

LESSONS FROM THE JUNKYARD

Have you ever achieved 100 percent of what you attempted as a leader? Your failure to do that doesn't mean you should attempt less—it means you should attempt more!

Think smart, come prepared, aim high, and don't be intimidated.

---

[5] Jesus tells his friends to be perfect (Matthew 5:48). Another example of aiming high?

3
RATS IN THE RAFTERS

Sometimes the solution is worse than the problem.

I was in seventh grade when Mom and Dad bought a run-down cattle ranch about thirty miles northeast of San Jose. Besides the sprawling but neglected ranch house, there were acres of rolling hills, fenced pastures, and decrepit fruit trees, along with a seasonal creek.

With just one brief excursion to Oklahoma, I had lived in San Jose all my life. But things were changing as I entered middle school, and not for the better (see chapter 8 about having friends in low places).

Dad wanted land and an escape from his daily junkyard routine. Mom wanted a real garden and fresh air. And twelve-year-old me was game to try anything.[1]

---

[1] Quite a change from the junkyard. Can you say culture shock? I went from greasy work boots to cowboy boots covered with, um, something else.

The ranch was perfect, apart from the approximately five bajillion ground squirrels already living there. These weren't cuddly Disney-style critters, mind you . . . they were vicious little critters. And in the absence of engaged owners, the squirrels had been running the ranch for years. They felt extremely entitled to the tunneled metropolis they'd excavated.

What they'd created *was* amazing, in its own way. Everywhere you looked—flat pasture, sloping orchard, creek banks, front yard—you saw holes. Infinite holes. The ranch was a rule-free paradise where the squirrels could dig to their little hearts' content.

Naturally, Dad decided to kill every last one of the buggers.

Not because he hated squirrels exactly, but more because he needed to protect our new herd of cattle. The cows weren't the smartest creatures to begin with, and when you add in spindly legs and gigantic torsos, tripping in a squirrel hole can amount to a death sentence for a cow or a huge vet bill for the owner.

Dad drove down to the Farm Bureau, and the good folks there supplied him with grain that was laced with a deadly poison. (Not just deadly to squirrels, either, but in 1972, that didn't seem to be on people's radar.)[2]

So Dad pastured all our livestock together in a safe spot and scattered that grain around as many holes as he could

[2] Okay, so it was on the radar for some people. The world owes folks like Rachel Carson a big debt. See Rachel Carson, *Silent Spring: The Classic that Launched the Environmental Movement* (New York: Houghton Mifflin, 2002).

find, and about two days later, squirrelpocalypse arrived. Not that *all* the squirrels suddenly vanished, but it made the problem manageable. Problem solved, with impressive results!

In our businesses and organizations, we often face a temptation immediately after achieving something impressive. We want to do it again. Replicate it immediately. Apply it to other situations.

And that's exactly what Dad did.

See, our wrecking yard had a similar problem. Instead of squirrels we had filthy rats, and instead of holes we had rafters. (And instead of livestock we had . . . junkyard customers. But that's taking the comparison too far. Probably.)

Rats in rafters weren't just bad because of the scurrying and gnawing and general mess. They also crapped on everything. Counters, customers, ledger books, the floor.

One Saturday, Dad lugged his leftover Farm Bureau grain down to the junkyard, scattered it around after work, and waited for the magic to happen.

Boy did it happen.

I know because I was working the shop the Monday after the poison kicked in. Like a normal Monday, the cavernous metal building smelled of oil, gasoline, and cigarette smoke. Dust and grime covered or coated nearly every surface. The employees arrived in various moods and states of alertness, and then customers showed up and began to browse the racks of parts.

Very much *unlike* a normal Monday, however, dead rats began to rain from the rafters.

Thwump. A nice fat rat keeled over on his rafter and plummeted down, down, down . . . right onto the back of Angel, who was leaning over the engine he was working on. I knew quite a few Spanish cuss words already, but apparently there were some I'd missed.

Thwump. Another bounced to the middle of the shop floor, just as a customer was walking through the front door.

Thwump. A third hit the countertop, right between the cash register and the phone.

On it went. Every single one of those critters had felt the need to eat the poisoned grain and then crawl all the way back up to the rafters before dying. Would it have killed them to just eat the grain and stay on the ground, hidden in the corners? Actually, it would have killed them, yes, but it would have helped us!

It rained rats for the rest of that day, and understandably, most customers fled.

The next day a few *new* customers came, specifically to see the dead rats. Let's just say that's *not* the kind of new customer you want.

Like poisoned rats, sales plummeted for a time. Once word of our *incident* spread among the other wrecking yards, the party-style phone lines we used to trade parts lit up with joke after joke after joke.

Yeah, any yards out there with an exhaust manifold that'll fit a '60 to '63 Lincoln Town Car . . . preferably without any dead rats clogging it up?

Hardy freakin' har har.

In a few short days, Dad had raced through all five of the emotional stages of rat exterminating:

Denial. Rat problem? What rat problem?
Anger. Wait, I have enough free poison to murder those little critters.
Bargaining. If rats stop falling from the rafters, I will never poison another fuzzy creature as long as I live.
Depression. Our yard is the laughingstock of California.
Acceptance. You know, this was pretty funny, I guess. Sort of.

The junkyard rats were dead, but in hindsight, Dad would have chosen to let them live. Poisoning the squirrels was a win. We got those holes filled in and let the cows out, and everyone was happy. (Except for the squirrels, of course.) Poisoning the rats was absolutely a loss. We killed the rats, but we hurt our business, too. And really, was the rat problem *so bad* that we needed to go nuclear on them? Sometimes a solution can be a lot worse than the problem.

SALVAGED FROM SCRIPTURE

The Bible contains a few cruel stories that can make us squirm—a bit like rat poison. The tale of David and Bathsheba (and Uriah) is certainly one of them—and the raw brutality of it can be lost if we skip straight to the moral.

So let's make sure we know the facts before drawing any conclusions. King David spies on Bathsheba—who happens to be married to one of his soldiers, Uriah—while she's taking a bath. David likes what he sees so much that he sends "messengers to get her" and bring her to the palace.[3] That adulterous one-night stand results in pregnancy. King David's solution? Murder Uriah. And this from one of our favorite Old Testament heroes, a "man after [God's] own heart."[4]

Talk about a solution that's a hundred times worse than the problem! (If you want to read the full story, by the way—and it's more brazen than this summary—check out 2 Samuel 11:1-27.)

Being a good leader can mean resisting the temptation to double down on our mistakes. It can also mean, as with my dad and the squirrel poison, resisting the temptation to apply a specific solution (reducing the squirrel population) more generally. I can say this for my dad's attempt to rid the junkyard of rats: At least he based his bad decision on the success of a previous decision. King David didn't even get that much right. He began with a bad idea when he caught a glimpse of Bathsheba, then compounded his mistake by "inviting" her over to the palace. David then made it even worse by failing to take responsibility for his actions. Oh, and I'm pretty sure having her husband killed earned David a mark in the negative column!

You have to admit: That's an impressive string of consecu-

---

[3] 2 Samuel 11:4. Doesn't sound like she had much of a choice.
[4] Acts 13:22, which is echoing 1 Samuel 13:14.

tive bad decisions! My dad learned his lesson after the rats started falling from the rafters, but King David didn't learn his until the prophet Nathan confronted him.[5]

In our businesses and churches and organizations, not every rat needs to be killed. Most of us should learn to live with a few rodent issues.[6]

Not every difficult customer, tense relationship, or supply-chain kink needs to be eliminated. Living with a problem is sometimes the wisest and most effective course of action. Not because the problem is so wonderful, but because eliminating the problem might spawn something even worse.

LESSONS FROM THE JUNKYARD

Sometimes a solution can be a lot worse than the problem.

Being a good leader can mean resisting the temptation to double down on our mistakes.

Living with a problem is sometimes the wisest and most effective course of action.

---

[5] See 2 Samuel 12 and Psalm 51.
[6] I know it's hard. I hate the idea too. But hey, you love Jesus, right? So suck it up.

4
BRING DONUTS
WHEN YOU'RE LATE
(AND DON'T BE LATE)

*We're always bringing donuts to God—and God is
always forgiving and putting us right back to work.*

In some ways, the junkyard is quite libertarian. Live and let
live . . . as long as all the parts get stacked, who cares how
you stack 'em. However, there is *one* absolute law of junkyard leadership never to be broken. One summer morning I
experienced it for myself.

When I woke, I knew instantly I was late for work. The
angle of the sun in my room was all wrong. I checked my
clock radio. Crap. Everyone at the yard would already have
been sweating away for almost an hour, and meanwhile the
owner's son was going to waltz in just in time for morning
break. Talk about bad optics.

Dad believed so strongly in personal responsibility that

he'd left for work without me. I pulled on the previous day's greasy jeans and a fresh T-shirt and tugged on my work boots. Two minutes later, I was sliding into the driver's seat of my rebuilt '70 Chevy Nova,[1] coaxing her to life and ripping down the driveway. I could be to the yard in twenty-five minutes, but I knew I had to make a detour. I went past my freeway exit and headed to Lincoln Avenue, pulled an illegal U-turn, and left my car running as I sprinted into Manley's Donuts.

I knew the deal. Show up late a few times and you might as well stay home because you'd be out of work. *Unless* you brought donuts. Late once, bring half a dozen. Late for the fifth time? Better bring a couple boxes! It was the absolute law of junkyard leadership that could not be trifled with: *Always* bring donuts if you're late.[2]

Ninety minutes after I was supposed to be at work, I walked through the wrecking yard door with a confident stride and a pink box held in front of me like an offering. I set the donuts on the counter, and without a word I started working.

Nobody said boo.

Isn't that an easy, graceful way to handle an issue like tardiness? We junkyard workers didn't have to do anything elaborate to make up for being late . . . but we had to do *something*. Even something as insignificant as a donut could become, in the junkyard economy, the currency of repentance.

---

[1] It was actually three cars cobbled together at the wrecking yard: a Buick Apollo in the back, a Chevy Nova in the front, and a bored-out big-block Chevy engine under the hood.

[2] One guy didn't show up for work for two days. We assumed he had skipped town or been arrested. But then he showed up (in a biblical way, on the third day), and he had four dozen donuts with him, enough for the entire crew and plenty left over for customers. It saved his job.

SALVAGED FROM SCRIPTURE

That's how God's economy operates too. In the Old Testament, if someone was too poor to sacrifice a lamb or a calf, they could instead sacrifice two doves.[3] Rich gift or poor gift, God forgave over and over. God provided access that didn't depend on social or economic status, but rather on willingness.

As someone who works for Jesus, I'm chronically late to work . . . and I'm *always* bringing donuts. Or at least I should be. Meaning whenever I show up to work, God's ready to give me my punch list for the day. I bring a small "sacrifice" to smooth things over. It could be almost anything, from a humble spirit to a prayer of confession to taking the time for a conversation. (Psalm 51 and Hosea 6 are good starting points for considering what the spiritual equivalent of donuts might be.)

God doesn't care exactly when we get to work, as long as we wake up eventually.[4] He wants us to get to work loving others and building his Kingdom, starting now.

We operate on a different plane than God. We're human, and when we interact with other humans we love and scream and forgive and ignore and resent and (hopefully) forget. It's all a big crapshoot, but at least donuts help sweeten our differences.

---

[3] Doves and pigeons are often used interchangeably in the Bible, but doves are mentioned more often. Imagine if the Holy Spirit had descended on Jesus like . . . a pigeon.

[4] Jesus told a parable about this, by the way, and it might be the Bible story most likely to give fits to businesspeople. Read the first chunk of Matthew 20 and see what you think.

LESSONS FROM THE JUNKYARD

Whenever I show up to work, God's ready to give me my punch list for the day.

God doesn't care exactly when we get to work, as long as we wake up eventually.

It's all a big crapshoot, but at least donuts help sweeten our differences.

5

THE NEGOTIATOR

*Smashing a radio can be a great way to build
your reputation as a tough negotiator—
especially if it's your own radio.*

One day, my uncle George was running the front counter at
Dad's wrecking yard when a customer came in looking for a
radio. Not just any radio, mind you, even though he could
have shoved about ninety-seven different kinds into that spot
in his early 60's Chevy Corvair.

No, the customer *had* to have an original Corvair radio—
and, of course, he wanted it at a cut-rate price. Our hotline
guy had already phoned around to find out which yards had
such a radio, and it turned out there was only one yard within
one hundred miles who had what the customer needed: us.

I watched from the end of the counter as Uncle George
returned to the cash register and set the radio down in front

of the customer. "Here it is, the *only* one around." He paused. "It's twenty-five bucks."

The customer allowed his eyes to bug out dramatically. "Twenty-five? Are you kiddin'? Twelve is more like it!"

Uncle George shrugged. "Twenty-five." The customer needed us more than we needed him, and my uncle knew it. This was going to be fun.

The customer patted the counter with his palms and sighed. "Aw, c'mon, George, you know this isn't worth more than fifteen. Be reasonable. You might have the only one, but that doesn't make it worth twenty-five bucks." This is where the customer blew it. He knew the radio was one of a kind, and he knew it was going to cost more than the average radio, but he wasn't willing to admit it. Thus he started at a ridiculously low price, only to raise it a few bucks. Both offers were insulting.

Even though I was only ten or so, I knew my uncle well enough to understand the look in his eyes. He'd hoped the customer would get the clear message that this wasn't really a bargaining session, given that the customer had zero leverage. Maybe if the customer had said twenty dollars, the conversation would have been more civil. But if the customer was going to keep pressing his luck, he'd end up pressing Uncle George into a foul mood.

My uncle told the customer in an *extremely* calm voice that the price was twenty-five dollars. The customer grew increasingly irritated. He pestered, whined, and pleaded for a lower price. And the whole time, the heat under Uncle

George was set to simmer. The customer didn't know it, but I did.

Finally, my uncle gave an ultimatum. "Look, *friend*, I'll say it one more time. The price is twenty-five bucks. Take it or leave it."

The customer rolled his eyes and threw up his arms dramatically. "But it's just not worth that, George, and you—"

In the blink of an eye Uncle George reached under the counter, grabbed a heavy mallet, and launched a full roundhouse swing at the radio.

Crash! Knobs, electrolytic capacitors, tubes, wires, scraps of metal . . . bits of the shattered radio launched in all directions.

Uncle George stared at the customer and asked, ever so calmly, "Now what'll you pay for it?"

Aghast, the customer spun around and stalked out the door. We could all hear him mumbling as he left about how crazy Uncle George was—and I suspected he was right!

At the time, my uncle's decision seemed irrational and even ridiculous. He irritated a customer *and* destroyed something that had value. Entertaining to be sure, but not a wise business decision.

Years later, I figured it out: Uncle George knew that the yard's reputation—and his reputation—was worth even more. Smashing that radio demonstrated he was unafraid to lose. He knew the story would spread far and wide, and for every person who decided not to get a part at "that crazy guy's junkyard" there would be nine people who'd (mostly unconsciously) pay

higher prices. Better to overpay a little than drag on the negotiation and have your beloved part destroyed!

SALVAGED FROM SCRIPTURE

An impetuous choice that causes short-term pain but builds
a long-term reputation as someone to be reckoned with?
That describes the apostle Peter, for sure. There are plenty of
examples to choose from, but think about the time the disciples cross the Sea of Galilee during a storm. They see Jesus
walking on water, and everyone but Peter has the appropriate
reaction: fear.

We can be so used to the rhythms of biblical language
that we forget the human story inside tame phrases. "They
were terrified," we read in Matthew 14:26. "'It's a ghost,' they
said, and cried out in fear." In other words, they were either
screaming, swearing, or trying to hide under the fishing nets.
Major freak-out time.

If you've ever inadvertently terrified a family member in
the middle of the night, you'll understand what Jesus does
next. Right away he tells them to take heart. It's him, not a
ghost. They don't need to be afraid.

Matthew's story doesn't tell us what the other disciples
make of this, but we know what Peter does. He comes right
back at Jesus and asks him to prove it. I imagine Jesus stifling
a smile. He's happy to prove it to Peter, but the proof Peter is
asking for—to be able to walk on water, and in the middle of
a storm, no less—is going to require serious chutzpah. Give

Peter credit, though. He climbs out of the boat, settles his feet on the water, and walks toward Jesus.

You probably remember what happens next. Peter is human. Like you, like me. He looks around and takes his eyes off Jesus. He realizes the relative safety of his boat is gone, and now it's just him trying to balance on a frothing surface of head-high waves. He begins to sink.

To Peter's credit, he immediately does the only thing that can save him: He cries out to Jesus for help.

When they're back on the boat, the storm dies down. Matthew's Gospel reports the awe of the disciples, who fall all over themselves proclaiming that *now* they're finally super-duper sure Jesus is God.

But I bet later, after they reached shore, they reserved some awe for Peter. "Dude, I can't believe you actually climbed out of the boat—what were you *thinking?*"

Would you pay twenty-five dollars for a reputation as someone who should never be crossed in a negotiation? Would you walk on water—or drown in the attempt—to prove a point?

Management gurus peddle the fiction that healthy negotiations can always be a win-win. That's false. *Most* of the time you can achieve a win-win, but on occasion that just isn't possible. When you find yourself in that situation, it's good to have a reputation as someone who's fearless, who will dare anything.

Sometimes you just have to smash a radio.

Sometimes you just have to step out of the boat.

LESSONS FROM THE JUNKYARD

Most of the time you can achieve a win-win, but it's good to have a reputation as someone who's fearless, who will dare anything.

Sometimes you just have to smash a radio.

6
ROLLS-ROYCE CAR POOL

Leaders ultimately are judged by their actions,
which Jesus teaches flow from the heart.

Some of the stuff that came out of my dad's junkyard would have made Dr. Frankenstein proud.

Like the Ford station wagon painted lime green—with a large plastic frog bolted to the top—that Little Bob entered in a destruction derby. Or the guy who bought a twelve-cylinder Jaguar motor to put in his Buick.

So I learned pretty quick not to judge junkyard things by their appearances—and not to judge junkyard *people* that way either.

With things, it was pretty easy. The tattered doorjamb plates were actually expensive aluminum, perfect for recycling. The catalytic converters, covered with road dust, were filled with precious metals like platinum. Even bald tires were of value to somebody, judging by how many were stolen when we set them out front.

Not judging people was a lot more difficult.

The eccentric customer who drove the old Studebaker filled with pizza boxes? He was actually a renowned rocket scientist working for General Electric down the road. And the Asian guy who barely spoke English and was missing an arm? He was a war hero to the thousands of Vietnamese refugees who had settled in our area.

So while it was tempting to judge them based on appearances, I had to learn it was wiser to judge less and observe more.

It reminds me of the time in elementary school when my best friend, Greg, and I got taken home in a Rolls-Royce.

Of course, in the days leading up to it, we bragged constantly, and none of our classmates believed us—at least until after school that day, when Mom pulled up at the wheel of a long, silver Rolls. Every kid ogled the new arrival. The long, elegant swoop of fender, flaring slightly above the back wheel. The impossibly long hood. The flying-lady hood ornament.

I opened the heavy, perfectly machined door and entered the spacious back seat. Greg followed, waving to our gasping classmates as we pulled away.

There was just one catch: Our wrecking-yard Rolls was running on a wrecking-yard Chevrolet engine.

Knowing the car was worth more in parts than whole, Dad had worked a deal with a local importer to pull the expensive Rolls-Royce engine out and replace it with a less expensive Chevy engine. All the looks and style of a Rolls, but *considerably* cheaper!

Most of us tend to look at the surface of things and make a quick judgment. And we're right *just* often enough to reinforce this practice as an easy way to navigate life. But it's often a trap. When we're too lazy to take time to look a little deeper, we can miss out on what's really going on.

No one is bothered when a Rolls runs on a cheaper engine, but people are a different story. As leaders—and as followers—we've got to look under the hood and learn what really powers the people around us.

SALVAGED FROM SCRIPTURE

Scripture actually talks about Chevy engines inside Rolls-Royce bodies quite a bit. Just as the engine is the heart of a car—and when you step on the gas it's the engine that responds, not the car's body—so the human heart is the source of our character and actions.

Remember when Samuel is tasked with picking the next king of Israel, and he assumes that whichever of Jesse's sons is the tallest and toughest will be God's chosen one? First Samuel 16:7 records the moment Samuel understands the parameters for the job search are divine, not human. "But the LORD said to Samuel, 'Do not consider his appearance or his height, for I have rejected him. The LORD does not look at the things people look at. People look at the outward appearance, but the LORD looks at the heart.'"

In the New Testament, Jesus instructs that "no good tree bears bad fruit, nor does a bad tree bear good fruit. Each tree is recognized by its own fruit. People do not pick figs from thornbushes, or grapes from briers" (Luke 6:43-44). Elsewhere, Jesus warns, "Watch out for false prophets. They come to you in sheep's clothing, but inwardly they are ferocious wolves" (Matthew 7:15).

We humans are obsessed with surface and appearance. Always have been, always will be. Godly leaders, however, must fight that tendency. As with the beautiful-looking Rolls-Royce with the Chevy engine, we need to ask what's under the hood.

Jesus makes the point explicit in Luke 6:45: "A good man brings good things out of the good stored up in his heart, and an evil man brings evil things out of the evil stored up in his heart. For the mouth speaks what the heart is full of."

My dad's Rolls-Chevy combo was pure fun. There were no harmful consequences from the fact that I got to cruise home from school in comfort. When it comes to leading, however, too many of us are like Rolls-Royce bodies pumping out Chevy-engine emissions. When our hearts are wrong, our leadership will always be harmed.

LESSONS FROM THE JUNKYARD

When we're too lazy to take time to look a little deeper, we can miss out on what's really going on.

As leaders—and as followers—we've got to look under the hood and learn what really powers the people around us.

We humans are obsessed with surface and appearance. Always have been, always will be. Godly leaders, however, must fight that tendency.

When our hearts are wrong, our leadership will always be harmed.

7

SMOKE-FILLED ROOMS

The best information is the hardest to get—but it's worth it.

The smoke-filled room. A cabal of power brokers convened around a table in an obscure corner of the building smoke cigars and trade off-color jokes as they secretly decide the fate of a candidate.

Perhaps that clichéd description doesn't describe reality as well as it did in days past, but every business has a smoke-filled room, at least metaphorically. It's the place where the best information trades hands. In some organizations, it might be as official as a boardroom, and in others, as informal as a golf course or the corner table of the nearby Starbucks. Make no mistake, though: Every organization has one.

Our junkyard actually had a *literal* smoke-filled room . . .

which just so happened to be our metaphorical smoke-filled room, as well.

Like every other wrecking yard, we had what was known as a "hot room": a tiny office barely large enough for a chair and a cheap desk. (This was how the rat insults arrived in chapter 3, where we called around for the Corvair radio in chapter 5, and so on.) My father chose one guy—usually the smartest and most aggressive employee, who was then paid on commission—to sit in that room all day, puffing cigarettes and talking or yelling on a bewildering variety of phones. The desk was covered with phones that were connected party-line style to a series of other junkyards, both near and far. Each hotline was set to speaker phone, meaning that whoever was behind the desk had instant access to a vast network of automotive information. One phone would be for a specific kind of car, for example, while another phone would be for junkyards within a ten-minute drive.

If a customer walked in and asked at the front counter for a right front fender for his '65 Mustang—and we didn't have one—we'd get on the hotline and ask. Every yard that did have one would chime in, along with the price they wanted. It became a bidding war at times. On the flip side, the guy in the hot room would hear dozens of other junkyards ask for parts their customers were searching for, and he could then respond if we had it in stock.

Having the best information meant succeeding as a business. The information let us move our inventory, retain customers, and occasionally outmaneuver other wrecking yards. Without that hot room, a lot of the customers asking for specific parts would have gone home disappointed . . . and might never have come back.

As a junkyard leader, my father knew the smart money was always in the smoke-filled rooms. Whichever guy worked those hotlines produced the best opportunities for the yard because he had access to the best information and the best network. The lesson I learned wasn't so much about management as it was about success. Find a way into that smoke-filled room. Even in a junkyard, access to knowledge combined with access to people was the key to success. Yes, hard work and intelligence were required. But without access to that hot room, hard work and intelligence had a ceiling.

Not much has changed. In nearly every business and organization today, success and failure often hinge on access to people and information.

SALVAGED FROM SCRIPTURE

Jesus says plenty of things that trouble us, assuming we take what he says at face value and refuse to spiritually neuter it. If an enemy takes your shirt, give him your jacket as well. It's easier for a camel to fit through the eye of a needle than for a rich person to enter the Kingdom of Heaven. Blessed are those who mourn. Love your enemies.[1]

---

[1] See Matthew 5:40, Luke 18:25, Matthew 5:4, and Matthew 5:44, respectively. And probably more, but you can find them on your own.

Or take Matthew 10:16: "I am sending you out like sheep among wolves. Therefore be as shrewd as snakes and as innocent as doves."

The junkyard-hotline operators knew that. They'd drive incredibly hard bargains . . . yet they relied on a network of personal relationships and even friendships. Broadly speaking, most of us could learn to operate more like that in our businesses and organizations. More subtly, most of us could make more of an effort to look for the untold story.

If you believe you've gathered all the facts you need by yourself, it's a safe bet you're going to miss out on information.

If you rely on others to voluntarily inform you of everything you need to know, it's a safe bet you'll be out of the loop at some point.

No matter how smart you are, and no matter how well connected you are, or how "open" your team is, there are conversations going on you don't know about. There are e-mails shared, looks exchanged, ideas considered—all happening outside the scope of your control or influence. There is always more information for us to uncover.

Do I sound cynical? I don't think so. Jesus said he was sending the disciples out like sheep among wolves. That's a tough balance to pull off, but it's worth it.

Accessing the smoke-filled room is a gritty and problematic reality for leaders who follow Jesus, but a reality nonetheless.

LESSONS FROM THE JUNKYARD

Success and failure often hinge on access to people and information.

If you believe you've gathered all the facts you need by yourself, it's a safe bet you're going to miss out on information.

If you rely on others to voluntarily inform you of everything you need to know, it's a safe bet you'll be out of the loop at some point.

8
IT'S GOOD TO HAVE FRIENDS IN LOW PLACES

Leaders love to have friends in high places—but friends in low places can make all the difference.

We've all heard the saying "It's good to have friends in high places." The junkyard turns that axiom upside down. In reality, it's good to have friends in low places—but note that I'm not equating *low* with lowly or unimportant!

Most of the folks I'm talking about are decent, good people, and they're just as important as anyone else. By "low," I mean their position on the organizational chart, or their relative power in society. Not too many bank presidents or bestselling authors or megachurch pastors walk around a junkyard or push forms back and forth across a desk at the DMV office. Of course, not everyone in a low place is decent by default either. Some are slimeballs, just as some people in high places are. But it's unquestionably true that most leaders could use more friends in low places rather than in high places.

I experienced this truth when I was still in elementary school. One day, I was walking home along Curtner Avenue,[1] minding my own business. I was bigger than average, so other kids typically didn't pick fights. That was fine by me, since I wasn't combative by nature. However, it's *possible* I had a smart mouth.

When I was angry or just wanted to tease, I could use my words to cut to the bone. Earlier in the week, I had irritated some boys at school who were older *and* significantly bigger. Bad idea.

They were waiting for me at the next intersection, three against one. There was no way I could outrun them, and no way I could outfight even one. So I did the only thing I could.

I insulted them.

Aaand . . . cue fight. It was just a kid fight—no weapons or anything really scary—but I was still getting pushed around pretty good. For every bruise I gave them, I got two or three in return. After a few frantic minutes, I ran out of energy. It was time to cover my head, hunch over, and try to avoid as many blows as possible before the boys gave up and left me alone. I was going to hear all about it at school for sure . . . and the way things were going, my mom was going to give me a lecture about my ripped clothes as well.

---

[1] Sadly, not riding in our Rolls-Royce. Mostly, Mom made me walk.

Suddenly, the ear-wrecking roar of a motorcycle blasted through the taunts and grunts. We all looked up just as a chopper braked to a stop at the curb. The bike was a gorgeous custom job complete with an outrageously long fork and an airbrushed American flag on its gas tank. The rider was a leather-clad man with a wild beard and flaming red hair. He idled his bike to *just* below the volume of a jet taking off.

"Hey! Roy! You okay?"

My savior was none other than "Insane Dwayne," one of our longtime junkyard employees and a family friend. He'd earned every bit of his nickname over the years. And by the time he spoke, one of the older boys had already taken off running.

I managed a smile. "Yeah, I think so!"

He revved his bike, and the other two boys scattered like leaves.

"Thanks, Dwayne!"

He grinned, then throttled back into traffic with just the hint of a cocky fishtail. Dwayne was cool enough to keep the incident to himself, and the bigger kids at school hassled me a *lot* less after word spread—and rumors grew—about my friend!

These days, when I'm heading off to meet with the latest "high" person, I no longer worry if I'll get physically pounded for my smart mouth . . . but if things get ugly, I still have Dwayne's number.

SALVAGED FROM SCRIPTURE

Rahab was a resident of Jericho. We're told she was a prostitute, but it might be better to think of her as a "madam." In our story, she has a level of power and autonomy, even though she operates her business in the gray-market economy. (You can read about her in Joshua 2 and 6.)

So the Israelite spies are scouting the Promised Land ahead of the main army. They sneak into Jericho ahead of the siege, hoping to assess the strength of the city. They end up hiding out at Rahab's brothel.

Unfortunately, everyone in town notices the two foreigners. The king promptly sends word to Rahab that she needs to give up the spies. But she's playing the long game. Rahab goes to talk to the spies first and says, "Look, everyone in town knows who has the winning hand here—your God is the one who's been slicing and dicing every enemy you've faced, starting with the pharaoh and ending with the Amorites. We know Jericho is toast, but I and my family don't have to be . . . right?"

A deal is quickly struck: If she helps the spies escape the city—and make no mistake, they'll be tortured and murdered if she doesn't—the spies will make sure she and her extended family are protected during the coming siege. She's a foreign enemy. A woman. A madam. Probably the only "lower" friend in town would have been a child. But what other options do they have?

That night, the Israelite spies do the old climb-down-the-rope-over-the-city-wall routine and eventually make their way back to the Israelite camp. Battle preparations are made. Then, just before the walls of Jericho are breached, Joshua, the commander of the Israelite army, gives final instructions to the warriors. "Remember, Rahab and everyone in her house will be spared."

After the battle, Rahab and her extended family are brought outside the ruins of Jericho, safe and sound—but it's partly because of Rahab that the Israelites won the battle in the first place. Now *that's* why you need friends in low places!

LESSONS FROM THE JUNKYARD

Most leaders could use more friends in low places rather than in high places.

Remember Rahab.

You need friends in low places![2]

---

[2] Elizabeth Symm, my wonderful copy editor, wrote the following comment on this point: "I'm suddenly reminded of Sherlock Holmes's homeless network, which I find brilliant." Brilliant indeed. Now I feel like Watson for not thinking of this sooner!

9
IMPORT/EXPORT

Leadership is never a popularity contest.

When I was seventeen, my dad put me to work at the front counter. The outside work, pulling parts and moving inventory around the yard, was a privilege reserved for the druggies, Hells Angels, guys without paperwork, and general rascals Dad didn't want interacting with customers.[1] And I didn't know enough—or chain-smoke enough—to operate the parts hotline. So my job was standard-issue customer service, except for the higher-than-average amount of grease and profanity.

One day, a guy sauntered in looking for some small part.

---

[1] Okay, they weren't *all* like that. Most were good hardworking folks. But who wants to read about that in a book about junkyards?

"I'm in imports," he said as we chatted. "Stuff from Taiwan, mostly."

Leaving me to wonder what exactly he imported. Kitchen appliances? Knockoff sunglasses? Something illegal? He never told me, and I didn't really care, because whatever he did, he was *cool*. Independent, ran his own business, traveled . . . he was living a life I could only dream of. And he still found time to talk to seventeen-year-old me.

Whenever he came in, we'd chat about cars or swap off-color jokes. He'd tell me stories about the import business, and I'd try to conjure up something of my own to brag about in return. And with every story, I found myself wanting more and more for him to like me.

One day, he came in looking depressed. "Roy, man, one of my guys ripped me off. Just took an entire pallet of inventory and split, you know? And the exchange rate is just *killing* me right now. It wouldn't be so bad if one of my main customers wasn't six weeks late on a payment."

I nodded my head sympathetically.[2] Maybe it wasn't as easy as I'd thought being an importer from Taiwan.

He leaned forward onto the counter and lowered his voice. "Roy, listen . . . can I get this transmission we've been talking about on credit, just this once?"

We *never* extended credit, and he knew it, which is why he told me right away that he was good for the money. He needed more time. He was working on some new angles that were about to pay off.

---

[2] And uncomprehendingly, if I'm being honest. That came back to bite me.

I didn't have to think much. He was an honorable guy who was down on his luck. If I were in his place, I'd want a favor too.

I agreed. And I never heard from him again.

When Dad found out, he brought it up on the way home. That thirty-minute drive was one of the times we could talk, though we were usually too tired to say much.

Dad asked why I'd broken the yard rules and extended credit, and because I was already feeling hurt—and defensive—I had a ready answer. "Well, it's good business to keep a good customer happy, right?"

Dad didn't say much, but I could tell he didn't exactly agree with my assessment.

"But all I wanted to do was help him out," I protested. "I was just trying to be a good guy."

"Roy, I don't think this was about you being a *good guy*. I think you wanted to be a *popular friend*."

Dad was wise enough to drive in silence for a while, which gave me the space to realize he was right. I'd been fooling myself. I hadn't wanted to do the right thing—I had just wanted an older, cooler guy to like me.

Dad let me look out the window while he said one more thing. "Remember, Roy, this isn't a popularity contest. There's nothing wrong with being a friend with customers or employees. There's nothing wrong with trusting. But you don't want to be driven by your desire to be popular. That'll get you into trouble. Eventually, you'll have to make tough decisions about some people, and if those decisions are driven by your desire to be liked, you're going to create a lot of pain for yourself . . . and do nothing to help the people around you."

Dad never busted my butt over the money. He knew the important thing was the bigger lesson. It was the first time I understood that a selfish motivation could hurt others. More than me got burned because I wanted to be liked: It was the whole yard. There was the lost money, sure, but there was lost trust as well. We'd been ripped off, and who knew how far the story would spread.

Since that afternoon, Dad's wisdom has proven true over and over. Chasing popularity is a good way to end up as the least popular person in the room. And doing the right thing will often make you unpopular. Whether in your business, your ministry, your family, or your friendships, you'll sometimes have to offend people if you want to do the right thing.

SALVAGED FROM SCRIPTURE

Removing the temptation of popularity from our decision-making is difficult but essential. It makes me think of when Jesus cleansed the Temple in Jerusalem. That's what our Bibles usually call it, but the reality was a lot messier. He didn't clean things up so much as shake things up. The courtyard was filled with merchants selling everything from cows down to pigeons. It was *supposed* to be a way for Jews to buy religious sacrifices, except greed got in the way. Worship had taken a back seat to profit. Even the guys selling pigeons—which were supposed to be a cheap-as-free sacrifice that even the poorest Jew could afford, like we talked about in the donut chapter—had jacked up the prices. The whole enterprise was sidetracked by salesmanship and exploitation, and Jesus was fed up. He rolled up his sleeves and became a holy wrecking crew: tables flipped, hawkers whipped, cages opened, piles of coins scattered across the courtyard.

By the time Jesus was done, it wasn't just the merchants who were incensed. The whole religious establishment was demanding answers. (Think of someone rampaging through a bustling trade show, destroying and denouncing everything in sight, if you want a modern comparison.)

But look what happens next in Matthew's version of the story: With all the sellers gone, the Temple courtyard finally has room for the blind and crippled, who Jesus begins to heal. And for children, who begin to run around shouting praise to Jesus.

That's when the priests turn purple with rage. Jesus is being simply *outrageous*, they say. He's destroyed legitimate businesses and introduced chaos to the holiest place in the country.

Know what? They were mostly right! But Jesus knew something the religious leaders didn't: that he was moving people closer to his Kingdom *through* disruption.

And he didn't give a fig for popularity.

I'm not Jesus. You're not Jesus. We can't afford to make unpopularity the *measure* of our actions. Some actions are unpopular because they're stupid or badly timed or selfish. Godly leaders can't act like jerks just for kicks.

But for every leader, there comes a time when making the right call means getting on the wrong side of popularity.

Some things you never forget. Like if you're a junkyard kid, you can always conjure up the smell of the Safety-Kleen solvent tank. Leadership lessons can be like that too. I'll never forget the moment I realized my "friend" had used me, and I'd let him because I wanted to be liked.

The good news is that if you *do* want to be popular all the time, all you have to do is never attempt anything important.

LESSONS FROM THE JUNKYARD

There's nothing wrong with trusting. But you don't want to be driven by your desire to be popular.

Whether in your business, your ministry, your family, or your friendships, you sometimes have to offend people if you want to do the right thing.

Jesus was moving people closer to his Kingdom through *disruption.*

SECTION TWO

OKAY, SO MAYBE I DIDN'T LEARN *EVERYTHING* I NEEDED TO KNOW ABOUT LEADERSHIP IN THE JUNKYARD.

10
QUESTIONING CAPTAIN SATELLITE

The best leaders ask the best questions at the best times.

Back in the 1960s, there was a show on KTVU-2 in Oakland called *Captain Satellite*. Bob March starred as the eponymous host, dressed in a helmet and a uniform with a streak of lightning across the chest. It was corny as all get-out, sure, but it was still must-see TV for every kid under the age of ten, including me.

The United States and the USSR were deep into the Cold War, much of which was being contested in outer space. The Soviet Sputnik satellite had shocked our nation a few years earlier, and now the challenge to put a man on the moon loomed large in people's imaginations. Nearly every American wanted to see it happen before the sixties ended, and massive resources—technology, military, government, engineering—were put into the effort. Kids across the nation were learning about rockets, Tang, and gravity. One obvious result was a widespread enthusiasm about space flight, which *Captain Satellite* tapped into.

So when I opened a letter addressed to *me*, from Captain Satellite, I was thrilled. One of my big sisters had sent in an application for me, and I'd been accepted to appear on the TV show. Soon the day of filming arrived, and Mom drove me to the soundstage in Oakland. When I stepped onto the set, my eyes widened—the *Starfinder II* felt like a real spaceship and not just a low-budget studio prop. And when Captain Satellite himself turned on the master generator so we could take off, I could almost convince myself we were flying. Not quite, since I could see my mom in the audience and all the cameramen working in the studio, but I wanted to believe it!

Partway through the broadcast, Captain Satellite told us we'd each have the chance to ask him one question. This was my moment! Not only would I get the chance to ask Captain Satellite something cool—and hopefully look smart and funny on television—but I'd also get a gift for participating. I'd seen some pretty great prizes handed out on the show before, and I imagined which one I'd get. Maybe it would be . . .

My thought trailed off. Suddenly I realized Captain Satellite was staring at me. So was the kid next to me. I tried to swallow, but my mouth was too dry. A question, a question, I needed to ask a question. My heart pounded in my ears.

Too late! The host's grin faltered a few millimeters as he turned to the boy beside me. The kid immediately asked, "How far away is the moon, Captain Satellite?"

I was shocked. That was *the* dumbest question he could have asked. There wasn't a kid in the country who didn't have the moon's distance memorized.

I mouthed the answer along with Captain Satellite. "238,900 miles." Maybe I'd get a chance to ask another question and impress everyone. Maybe I'd . . . nope. Too late. The theme music kicked on, the studio audience applauded, aaaand *cut!* The show was over.

Minutes later, we kids lined up to get a keepsake: Captain Satellite's signature on a map of the solar system. The kid in front of me was the one who had asked the stupid question, and Captain Satellite gave him a small globe of the moon. I practically started drooling. I had one last opportunity to make up for my failure. I stood in front of the table. "Captain Satellite," I asked, "do you really think we'll get to the moon this decade, or is it just too much of a challenge?"

Now that *was a darn good question,* I thought. I allowed myself a small smile.

But the captain didn't even look up as he scrawled his signature across the solar system. "Of course," he answered in a bored monotone. "Smart people are working on it."

That was it. No detailed answer. No moon globe. Not even any eye contact. Two minutes later, I was slumped in the back seat of Mom's car, driving home.

My question *had* been a good one, but I had missed my

chance to ask it in the right context. As leaders, we can't afford to assume we know everything, so we need to ask the right questions. Perhaps even more important, however, is asking them at the right times. Knowing when to ask—often well in advance of when we need the answer—is critical.

Sometimes we are overwhelmed with nerves and fail to ask the right question, like my younger self on a TV stage that looked like a spaceship. My biggest mistake was not having my question prepared in advance. It was a mistake. Okay, so it was a mistake made by a starstruck little boy on live television, but still, it was a mistake.

Asking good questions is a learned skill. We can all become better at it. One simple way to improve is to think strategically about who to ask, when to ask, and how to phrase our question. Too often, we ask our questions of the wrong person, which just triangulates conversations and wastes time. Other times, we ask at the wrong moment. And of course, it's important to phrase our question properly, so it is genuine, thoughtful, and nonthreatening and conveys a constructive tone.

Will we fail in our attempts to ask good questions? Definitely. But far worse is to fail to ask them in the first place.

SALVAGED FROM SCRIPTURE

I love how Moses isn't afraid to question God at the burning bush.

In Exodus 3, we read about how Moses is working as a

shepherd out in the boonies. One day, he sees a burning bush that isn't burning up, so he heads over to investigate—only to have God speak directly to him from within the fire. Moses freaks out but eventually calms down enough to listen. God tells Moses the plan: In order to rescue God's people from slavery in Egypt, God is going to send Moses to speak with Pharaoh. Instead of sprinting off toward the palace in the city, however, Moses ends his temporary silence by asking God a series of questions.[1]

Why are you choosing me for this job?

What if the Israelites ask me your name, God? What should I tell them?

What if they don't listen to me, and what if they say I made up the whole God-in-a-burning-bush thing?

Then something occurs to Moses, and he brings it up with God. No time like the present, right? "Also, God, it turns out I'm not a good public speaker, so . . ."

After all this questioning, God gets angry with Moses and tells him to get on board with the plan. Still, you have to admire Moses for having the guts to ask. And his "boss"—or Boss would be more accurate—was patient for a long conversation. We probably don't want to hold this story up as

---

[1] Okay, total aside. I was in Egypt recently and visited Mount Sinai. At the bottom of the hill is a monastery, Saint Catherine's, that was established almost fifteen hundred years ago. And the monks insist that the large bush in their courtyard is *the* burning bush Moses saw. Hmmm . . .

a *model* exactly, but it is thought-provoking. The trouble is that pestering God with genuine questions can easily slip into procrastination or even disobedience.

At least in part, however, Moses was trying to wrap his brain around what it meant to follow God. Every question he asked—and God answered—gave him a better picture of what would be expected of him. If Moses was going to lead the Israelites, he first needed to ask the right questions at the right time.

LESSONS FROM THE JUNKYARD

Knowing when to ask—often well in advance of when we need the answer—is critical.

Asking good questions is a learned skill. We can all become better at it.

11

GAMBLING ON ANSWERS

Leaders can't afford to assume they know all the results of their actions.

Once upon a time, my parents owned a vacation home in South Lake Tahoe—but that didn't mean Dad left his penny-pinching ways back in San Jose. If we ever went out for dinner on those vacations, it was to one of the cheap buffets at the casinos just across the state line in Nevada. Dad thought gambling was a complete waste of time, utterly at odds with good business sense. Only a sucker would play on another man's terms instead of his own. But that was no reason to avoid the cheap food!

One vacation, when I was in grade school, I found myself in yet another buffet line, wondering how many scoops of chocolate pudding I'd be allowed to shovel on my plate. Dad tapped my shoulder to get my attention.

"Roy," he said, reaching into his pocket and pulling out a nickel, "let me teach you a lesson."

The nearest slot machine was so close Dad didn't need to step out of line. He dropped in the nickel, pulled the lever, and taught me a lesson I've never forgotten.

The dials on the slot machine spun . . . slowed . . . stopped one by one . . . *ding ding ding!* Everyone within hearing distance turned to look. Dad had hit a jackpot! Coins began to flood the catch tray, making such a racket I could barely hear Mom's incredulous laughter.

Dad could only stare, dumbfounded.

"Wow, Dad!" I gushed. "What a *great* lesson! Can you teach me that lesson again?"[1]

Eventually, Dad laughed too, but with a touch of embarrassment. (The embarrassment did not prevent him from paying for dinner with a boatload of nickels, however.) That unexpected jackpot instantly became part of Goble family lore. I even laughed about it recently with my mom, who is now ninety-four. I've reflected on that moment over the years, and just as Dad intended, it really did teach me a lesson.

Not, of course, that gambling never pays. That day it obviously *did* pay. Neither was it the opposite (and wrong) lesson that gambling is worthwhile. I gave my dad a hard time, but even as a kid, I knew how lucky he'd gotten, and that if we put every one of those coins back into the slot machine we'd eventually lose them all. The reason "The

---

[1] What can I say? I was born a smart aleck.

house always wins" is an axiom is because . . . the house always wins.

Rather, the lesson I learned was about leadership. We can't control what we don't know, but sometimes we can't even control what we *do* know.

Litigation attorneys have a rule when examining a witness in court: Never ask a question if you don't already know the answer. Why? Unexpected answers can flip a trial on its head. Wise attorneys ask their questions in deposition, away from the jury and judge, then attempt to guide the witnesses to a desired conclusion.

Dad's method of buffet-line teaching contained an inherent risk. He bet, literally, that he wouldn't win his bet! When you play the odds, sometimes the odds play you instead.

SALVAGED FROM SCRIPTURE

James knew about playing the odds—and getting played.

> Now listen, you who say, "Today or tomorrow we
> will go to this or that city, spend a year there, carry
> on business and make money." Why, you do not even
> know what will happen tomorrow. What is your life?
> You are a mist that appears for a little while and then
> vanishes. Instead, you ought to say, "If it is the Lord's
> will, we will live and do this or that." As it is, you boast
> in your arrogant schemes. All such boasting is evil.
>
> JAMES 4:13-16

That's safe, right? We can nod our heads and be pious about that verse, tacking on "if it is the Lord's will" to whatever we already plan to do!

But think about the story of Stephen's death in Acts 6–7. The young church is starting to spread like crazy, and one of its most gifted leaders gets in trouble because jealous rivals lie about him. He's dragged before a court to explain himself—even though the charges are false—and all of a sudden, he gets fired up by God's Spirit. Instead of defending himself, he absolutely *rips* into the gathered officials. It would be like if I was accused of shoving an old lady, and in my defense, I repeatedly punched her in the face.

Stephen ends up making the officials so angry they stick their fingers in their ears, shout him down, drag him outside the city, and stone him. (Quick aside: Stoning was not a good way to go. It takes long enough to die from blunt force trauma that the victim can be conscious for some time. Stephen was, and he prayed for the people who were murdering him. I don't know about you, but I would . . . not have been praying for them.)[2]

To recap, Stephen does what he thinks he's supposed to do, and he does it extremely well. He literally gives the best sermon of his life, and in front of a hostile crowd, no less. The result? Stephen dies, and the church is immediately forced to flee across the known world and beyond. Stephen didn't know that would happen, and neither did any of the

---

[2] Bonus: The apostle Paul—but back when he was still a jerk named Saul—watched the execution with a satisfied grin.

disciples. It worked out well, of course: The church spread across the known world. But it was also a time of great uncertainty and fear as the authorities began to aggressively persecute the young church.

It's a lesson to take to heart. We think we can control things. As leaders, we even make bets assuming we can. But managing a situation, controlling the flow of an endeavor, is a human ambition that can often be self-delusional. Sometimes, life acts like a slot machine, and remembering that can help keep us humble when unexpected lessons land in our laps.

LESSONS FROM THE JUNKYARD

Sometimes, we can't even control what we do know.

When you play the odds, sometimes the odds play you instead.

Managing a situation, controlling the flow of an endeavor, is a human ambition that can often be self-delusional.

12

PROFANITY MUST BE EARNED

Unless you've earned the right to use profanity, using it to make your case with people you lead is going to backfire.

During my teen years, it would have been accurate to label me—in my mother's preferred phrase—a "potty mouth." That was unsurprising, given that the guys I worked with in Dad's wrecking yard were more like porta-potty mouths, or even sewer mouths.[1] By age seventeen, when I went on my first date with D'Aun, my language hadn't exactly improved. Which was unintentionally fortunate, because I'd been given a pair of tickets to go see George Carlin perform his infamous "Seven Words You Can Never Say on Television" routine at the Circle Star Theatre in San Carlos.

---

[1] The publisher wouldn't allow me to use light profanity in this book. My argument was that for every Christian bookstore reader I lost, I might gain one or two readers who don't consider Precious Moments figurines expressions of Christian faith. But I was overruled.

71

(Are you wondering where this is going? Hang in there—we'll get to leadership real soon.)

I'd known D'Aun ever since eighth grade. She was gorgeous, popular, and friendly and always seemed to be smiling. In other words, *way* out of my league. We technically ran in the same circle of high-school friends, but *technically* Earth and Jupiter both orbit the sun. Doesn't mean they're going to get together anytime soon.

Still, a little voice in my head suggested, *Why not ask her to go with you?* So I did. And she said *yes*!

(I don't remember being nervous. Then again, I don't remember anything about that moment. Which probably means I was so terrified, I repressed the whole event.)

Finally, the night of our first date arrived. I picked up D'Aun in my Mustang with the racing-stripe paint job. We drove to Fremont, which was the only city between Pleasanton and the Circle Star Theatre that I knew my way around. I classed things up by choosing a Lyon's Restaurant—think Denny's, except bankrupt now. At least it was away from the neighborhoods we usually frequented, meaning no one would see us. I didn't spill anything, D'Aun didn't ignore me, and before long, we were off to our show.

You've probably heard about Carlin's classic routine. It's almost quaint by the foul-mouthed standards of many of today's comics, but at the time it was plenty edgy.[2]

---

[2] The words, in case you're interested, are _____, _____, _____, _____, _____, _____, and _____. If these lines are blank, you can thank NavPress. Or my mother.

I just about died laughing—and I knew I *really* liked D'Aun when I realized she was laughing as hard as I was. A nearby couple, who I will generously describe as prudish, were *not* enjoying Carlin's jokes, which of course made D'Aun and me laugh that much harder![3]

I tell this story because my seventeen-year-old self, if he could see me now, might think of me as a bit prudish. Unlike that couple near us in 1975, I would certainly still laugh at Carlin's routine, but my younger self would be surprised by how infrequently I swear these days.

What changed me was an interaction about a decade after my first date with D'Aun. The church plant D'Aun and I were involved with had purchased a building, and I was asked to help oversee the interior construction. The project wasn't anything terribly fancy—basically just adding a few interior walls and some amenities to a small commercial building—but someone needed to bird-dog the subcontractors and church volunteers. One day, a guy from the city showed up to inspect the rough plumbing in our new bathroom. He pointed out a million things we'd done wrong, and he chose to be maximally pushy and condescending about it. Guys from the church had done all the work, and I had no idea if the inspector was even correct, but I had to stand there while he reamed me out for what seemed like an eternity.

The moment the door shut behind him, I absolutely lost

---

[3] Some readers will want the rest of the story. I drove the long way back to Pleasanton because I didn't want the evening to end. Eventually, however, we found ourselves face-to-face in front of her front door. Our first kiss. Magic. Five years later I proposed. Now we've been married nearly four decades. The joy of that first kiss is still with us today. It set the course of our histories, and I thank God daily for D'Aun.

it. Who did this guy think he was? We were volunteers learning how to build a church bathroom, for Pete's sake, not professional plumbers working on a new hospital. Sure, we wanted to get it done right, but seriously? Why be so pathetically pushy about it? I vented like a volcano, swearing a blue streak about bureaucrats, construction workers, and government red tape.

Did I mention our pastor was there? Fortunately, he played it cool and laughed off my tirade. Which gave me the space to realize something about myself: In what amounted to a church, I had gone full junkyard mouth. About a plumbing inspection. Was that the kind of guy I wanted to be?

I pledged to change, simple as that. And I did.[4]

I took out most of the profanity from my vocabulary because it seemed like the wiser way to live. I still swear, but far less than I used to—and I pay much more attention to context. Although a trusty four-letter word is sometimes the best expression I can muster, it's a rarity now compared to the old days.

Which brings me to a rant—and brings *us* to the topic of leadership. Lately, I've noticed an awful lot of swearing that is absolutely inappropriate. It's coming from younger leaders, certain political types, and CEOs trying to relate to their teams. It's even coming from "hip" pastors and church leaders. There's a generation of leaders swearing up a storm, trying to make themselves appear to be something they are

---

[4] Boring pivot, I know. But we can simply change in more areas of our lives than we sometimes admit. Not everything has to be a process or complicated.

not. They want to seem grittier, or more authentic, or less bound by so-called social conventions and pressures.

And they're trying *way* too hard.

See, after growing up in the junkyard, and then living for decades in the worlds of construction, international non-profits, underfunded education, and the rollicking petty squabbles of the local church, I can state that profanity must be earned . . . and very few people have earned the right to use it.

When your life is neatly packaged and safe, profanity only serves to make you appear lame. If you're sitting in your air-conditioned office, and the intern brings you the wrong drink from Starbucks, you don't get to swear. You just don't. Or if you just signed the paperwork on a nasty corporate takeover, and you want to rub it in the face of the loser across the conference table, you can't suddenly start swearing like a sailor. For that matter, if you're a weekend sailor, you prob-ably shouldn't be cursing a blue streak either.

But if you're the mechanic who goes home with grease under his fingernails? Or the ER nurse with bloodstains on her smock, or the army sergeant responsible for the lives of a platoon, or the one who picks up somebody else's garbage all day? Yeah, you've earned the right to some colorful language. Those who deal with the caustic, corrosive aspects of life, and those who understand the daily sweat of grinding out a paycheck, they're the ones who can choose to speak in a way that would—or should—make the rest of us squeamish.

The point here is obvious but important: Unless you've

earned the right to use profanity, using it to make your case with people you lead is going to backfire. They'll see right through your posing, find you laughable, and tune you out. They'll consider you unserious for not using more descriptive, accurate, and helpful words. A few will be truly offended, and your lack of concern for their offense will push them further away from you. You will not look tough by using profanity any more than you will look prudish for avoiding it.

If you're constantly cursing, you will, in short, be a lousy leader who can never inspire higher than the gutter of your mouth. Instead, keep your verbal powder dry for when you really need it. If you haven't earned the right to be profane when necessary, no amount of superfluous swearing is going to make anyone believe you're anything better than an old-fashioned jerk.

So if you catch yourself swearing in front of others just for the sake of appearances, you should really . . . well, just shut up.

(Rant over. I feel much better now.)

SALVAGED FROM SCRIPTURE

The story is too good not to quote. In my experience, people who don't already *know* this is part of the Bible have a hard time believing it.

> From there Elisha went up to Bethel. As he was
> walking along the road, some boys came out of the

town and jeered at him. "Get out of here, baldy!"
they said. "Get out of here, baldy!" He turned
around, looked at them and called down a curse
on them in the name of the LORD. Then two bears
came out of the woods and mauled forty-two of the
boys. And he went on to Mount Carmel and from
there returned to Samaria.

2 KINGS 2:23-25

Man, I *love* that story. The Bible is way wilder than we
like to admit. Way more *human*.[5]

Many points could be made from this passage—so many,
in fact, that you might want to ask your pastor to preach on
it. My point is that these young punks hadn't earned the right
to curse and mock Elisha. (Actually, *nobody* had earned that
right.) They might not have even earned the right to shave!
However, they paid for their casual use of coarse language
when two bears showed up to teach them some "manners."

Elsewhere in Scripture, though, great leaders sometimes
employ off-color language for a higher, redeeming purpose.
A few of these stories are elsewhere in the book, like Paul
telling others to emasculate themselves,[6] or admitting everything else he possesses is excrement in the gutter compared
to Jesus.[7] Unlike those luckless boys whose casual profanity
brought them to a close encounter with two angry bears, Paul

---

5 Have I considered calling wild bears to attack my persecutors? Yes, on occasion.

6 Don't believe me? Check out Galatians 5:12.

7 Still don't believe me? Well, read Philippians 3:8.

had certainly earned the right to go off every now and then. How many times was he beaten, shipwrecked, chained, or imprisoned?

I'm enough of a Protestant to know we don't earn grace. But we sure have to earn our right to use profanity.

LESSONS FROM THE JUNKYARD

You will not look tough by using profanity any more than you will look prudish for avoiding it.

If you're constantly cursing, you will be a lousy leader who can never inspire higher than the gutter of your mouth.

Keep your verbal powder dry for when you really need it.

13
A FLAMETHROWER AND IMMUNITY

A good leader sometimes says things to make people uncomfortable in order to galvanize action.

Our family wrecking yards weren't easy on the eyes . . . or really, on *any* of the senses. There were mounds of rusting vehicles, wind-whipped dust devils, heavy foot and vehicle traffic, chemical and mechanical odors, the screech of metal being pulled apart, and even literal junkyard dogs growling and barking.[1]

All of which must have stunk for the mobile-home park directly next door.

It was an idiotic location for a residential neighborhood in the first place, but that was how San Jose rolled in the

---

[1] Okay, so honestly, our junkyard dogs tended to just wag their tails. My dad used to say they'd probably hold the flashlight for a thief.

act-more-think-less years right after World War II. If you wanted to build something, you just built it, even if it meant plopping down a hundred mobile homes in a place guaranteed to produce plummeting property values and attract the worst sort of residents. The park was a nice place to live for a handful of years, and then it began its inevitable descent. The narrow streets and run-down subleased single-wides became a home of last resort for most who lived there. Mixed in with some hardworking people who never caught a break were car thieves, drug dealers, and a high-profile child abuser.

The people in that mobile-home park needed a fresh start, and the park itself absolutely needed to be shut down. The criminal elements didn't deserve a base of operations, and the remaining reputable folks deserved a quiet home somewhere with a lot fewer police sirens.

By the mideighties, I was running Goble Properties, our family real estate venture, and we proposed a solution: We'd buy the property, relocate the tenants at our cost, remove the mobile homes, and build new housing, commercial buildings, landscaping, and lighting, along with a host of other improvements. The redevelopment would be a massive upgrade for that area of San Jose, and it would turn us a profit. It was a classic win-win.

Naturally, the city changed its zoning rules *right* after we purchased the property. Shutting down a mobile-home park had previously required sending eviction notices, waiting 120 days, helping the residents find new housing, and then sending in the bulldozers. Thanks to the updated rules, which were a well-intentioned attempt to protect residents, our project would drown in an ocean of red tape.

My attorney and I asked for a meeting with the city planners. It was obvious the city wanted our project to move ahead, but their hands were tied by their own rules. The situation was frustrating, unnecessary, and just plain stupid. I became increasingly exasperated.

There was a city councillor at the meeting, and he asked, "Mr. Goble, what do you need from us to close this park?"

I didn't miss a beat. "Immunity and a flamethrower."

The city councillor stared at me incredulously, as if he couldn't believe what I'd just said. The eyes of the two city employees widened in shock. My attorney's heart probably skipped a beat or two, but I got my point across—and more importantly, I grabbed everyone's attention and focused it on solving the matter at hand. (Which we did. The rest of the story is quite boring, but our project was approved in the end.) Leadership can require stepping on a few toes—or breaking a few norms—in order to move things forward. Politeness has its place, but sometimes, so do flamethrowers.

SALVAGED FROM SCRIPTURE

The apostle Paul sometimes used vivid language. He was a feisty sort anyway, and his conversion from bounty hunter to church planter didn't do much to soften his edge.

In his letter to the Galatians, for example, Paul gets so fed up with his opponents that he fumes, "As for those agitators, I wish they would go the whole way and emascu-late themselves!" (Galatians 5:12). That's the kind of phrase a modern reader can sometimes skim over—intentionally or not—without paying attention to the fact that Paul is talk-ing about his enemies cutting off their own genitalia. Paul is using emphatic, uncomfortable language for a beneficial reason.

Can we add this to our own leadership arsenals? Asking for a flamethrower and immunity wasn't what the people at the meeting wanted to hear. Truthfully, it wasn't what they *needed* to hear, at least in one sense, because I wasn't actually proposing a solution. In another sense, though, I refocused the conversation and let them know that it might be time to move past niceties and explore creative ways to move for-ward. If we speak this way all the time, we'll lose our ability to shock for the right reasons. If we choose our moments, how-ever, a well-timed verbal bomb can make all the difference.

LESSONS FROM THE JUNKYARD

Leadership can require stepping on a few toes—or breaking a few norms—in order to move things forward.

Politeness has its place, but sometimes, so do flamethrowers.

A well-timed verbal bomb can make all the difference.

14
GETTING THE RIGHT PEOPLE ON THE BUS

Sometimes the right people on the bus are the wrong people.

Jim Collins writes great business books.

I want that to stand as its own paragraph because I'm about to pivot to a giant *however*. Collins truly has helped countless leaders explore new ideas, think more carefully, and manage more effectively. I admire and respect him and his work.

However, his ideas are often presented so memorably and so simply that they become . . . simplistic. The issue is mostly with readers, rather than Collins's texts, which are generally wise and nuanced. Readers don't tend to discuss the rich subtleties of Collins's latest book, though; instead, they settle for sharing only one or two ideas—and sometimes only the title![1]

---

[1] Jim Collins, *Good to Great: Why Some Companies Make the Leap . . . and Others Don't* (New York: HarperBusiness, 2001). I talk more about this in chapter 15.

For instance, nearly every leader has heard Collins's maxim that we need to get "the right people on the bus."[2] Most of us understand it to mean that if we want our organization to succeed, we need to hire the right people for the right jobs. Once they are in positions that maximize their strengths and minimize their weaknesses, organizational success will be orders of magnitude more likely.

Get the right people on the bus—that sounds great!

Except it doesn't actually make sense. Or it doesn't make the kind of simple, universally applicable sense we *want* it to make.

First, it's far easier to *talk* about getting the right people on the bus than it is to hire and retain them. Some are happily employed elsewhere. Some command higher salaries than we can afford. We can't instantly hire and fire people—and even if we had that power, there would be countless moral and practical complications.

Second, it's tempting to think "right" means "best"—but it doesn't. None of us will ever have a pure all-star team. There will always be someone somewhere who is brighter, more talented, harder working, and so on. And we will always have a few utility players (to stretch the sports analogy further) who aren't elite but are nevertheless quite valuable.

Finally—and this is the most important point— sometimes, our job is to work with the "wrong" people on the bus. Generally, Collins (like most business writers)

---

[2] Jim Collins, *Good to Great*, 13. It is, ahem, a good book.

defines success as organizational success. That makes sense in the context of his books. But what about in the context of your organization: Is the well-being of the organization the only metric you use to define success?

I see my coworkers as flawed works in progress, *and I'm sure they see me the same way.*

None of us is perfect. None of us gets it right every single time. Working alongside imperfect people takes more time and energy than working alongside the best employee possible for that position. It's a drain on resources. It hurts the bottom line. For me, however—and if you're still reading the book at this point, then for you, as well—the organization is not the only thing that matters. Sometimes, the right people on the bus are the ones who need us more than we need them.

Some companies are ruthless about putting the right people on the bus, often producing astounding financial results. But guess what happens when you're the A-lister on the bus and along comes an A-*plus*-lister? Next thing you know, the bus is disappearing in a cloud of exhaust. (Or in a cloud of rainbows and butterflies, if it belongs to an eco-friendly tech company.)

I'd rather look at the people on my team, try to understand their strengths and weaknesses (and mine as well!), and invest in their lives. This means more time spent serving colleagues and less time serving my organization—and that's the point. Ten years from now, I should care less about the organization and more about whether the people God has placed in my life are thriving.

I'm not naive. Businesses and nonprofits and churches need to pay bills and retain staff. Businesses need to be profitable if they want to keep the lights on. Nonprofits need to keep operating if they want to have an impact. Churches need to wean themselves from "sloppy agape"[3] in their management. These needs are ever present.

But my modest suggestion is that we guard against a cavalier entitlement to kicking people off the bus—and a shallow fixation with only having the right people on the bus.[4] Investing in the team you have, rather than the team you *wish* you had, is a basic leadership principle—just like it's foundational to following Jesus.

If following Jesus is our ultimate goal, then let's not allow our enthusiasm for achievement to overpower our God-given mandate to be known by our love.

SALVAGED FROM SCRIPTURE

Some of my Scripture applications have been creative, I'll admit—but some write themselves! Which of the twelve disciples would *not* have been kicked off the bus if Jesus had read a blog about Jim Collins during one of his morning solitude sessions? Let's see . . .

---

[3] *Agape* means love, of course. Sometimes, churches get sloppy in their management style, not wanting to offend a colleague or create tension. It often results in a passive-aggressive management style that makes everything, well, sloppy.

[4] I suspect Collins would agree with this, by the way. In leadership, as in politics and so many other arenas, sound bites are easier than substantive decision-making.

Judas. A no-brainer, since he took trade secrets to a direct competitor.

Simon the Zealot. Let's just say anti-government plotters don't make the best colleagues.

Thomas. Clearly needed to trust the program more.

James and John, the sons of Zebedee. Asked for a wildly inappropriate promotion. And they had to be Millennials, since they kept bringing their mother to work.

Matthew the tax collector. An active member of an international money-laundering scheme.

Peter. Denied his CEO in three separate on-the-record interviews.

Maybe Jesus would have kept the rest, just because they didn't screw up quite as much!

Scripture is filled with such examples. Although there are obviously some amazing men and women in Scripture, almost all had traits that would look devastatingly bad during their job review. Something to remember the next time you meet with your coworkers!

LESSONS FROM THE JUNKYARD

The organization is not the only thing that matters.

Ten years from now, I should care less about the organization and more about whether the people God has placed in my life are thriving.

Investing in the team you have, rather than the team you wish you had, is a basic leadership principle—just like it's foundational to following Jesus.

15
GOOD TO GREAT?

Good to great often isn't.

When my son Jedd was just out of college, we were cleaning the old family ranch house. He brought me a briefcase he'd found in one of the rooms. Looking a bit like an accountant—which did *not* reflect his current career as an app developer—he tossed the briefcase on the counter and asked, "Can I open it?"

"Go ahead. I think it belonged to your grandpa Goble."

He popped the clasps, lifted the lid, and . . . sunglasses. It was *full* of cheap sunglasses. Dozens of them. All exactly the same style and brand. And suddenly, I remembered the time I'd asked Dad to share his business philosophy.

We had been standing at the front counter at the junkyard,

and there was a lull between customers and tasks. He didn't answer me right away, probably because he was struggling to put words to a concept he'd always intuited but never articulated.

"I think of business as standing before a table filled with good things," he started. Then he opened his arms wide. "I stretch out my arms and embrace all that I can possibly reach. I don't worry about quality."

Then came the kicker. "Just get the job done."

Which is why he was the kind of leader who'd buy cheap sunglasses in bulk. Maybe he always looked the same, but if he lost a pair—which he frequently did—so what? He'd grab another and get on with whatever needed doing.

That practical (and necessary) "get 'er done" attitude is all too hamstrung by our desire to be great. We all know the phrase "good to great," taken from the Jim Collins book of the same name. As with our last chapter, I appreciate Collins's message, but it's been misunderstood in ways that harm leaders.

How? In the sense that far too many phonies with far too high an opinion of themselves have taken the title—*Good to Great*—and decided it describes everything they might do. Everything they *should* do. Great from sunup to sundown. Great 24-7-365.

Give. Me. A. Break.

If *everything* is great, nothing is great. Great is relative. Basketball superstar Stephen Curry is considered great because most other NBA players *aren't* great, at least compared to him. Does that mean the NBA as a whole doesn't entertain fans or produce the best basketball on the planet? Absolutely not. Does that mean Curry is always great? Nope—he has off nights, just like anyone else.

In fact, I'll go so far as to say that if we want to be better leaders, we should worry a whole lot less about going from good to great. Instead we should chill out more.

Embrace "good enough" and "got the job done."

Focus on simplicity and reliability.

Get comfortable with competency.

The less-than-sexy truth about leadership is that most of the world, most of the time, runs on *competency*, not greatness. Greatness does exist. We should strive for greatness when appropriate. But most of the time, getting the job done is good enough.

But wait: If we pursue greatness *less*, would that make us below-average leaders? Folks failing to live up to our potential?

I'm tempted to answer that with something wise and self-deprecating, but instead I'll go with an emphatic *Nah!*

In reality, consistent *goodness*, rather than greatness, is certainly healthier for most people, in most situations, most of the time.

The trouble with *always* pursuing greatness is that it forces us to focus on the wrong goals. It tempts us to be narcissistic. It invites us to sink too much time and energy into too few things. The desire for greatness can make us competitive with each other. And when we obsess about those kinds of things instead of the simple daily chores that keep our business or church functioning? We become the wrong sort of leaders.

SALVAGED FROM SCRIPTURE

In Luke 7, we meet a nameless Roman soldier. Read the whole chapter for yourself later—or now . . . God knows it's more important than this book you're holding.

In this passage, we're introduced to a centurion who's just another anonymous cog in the vast machinery of Pax Romana. If you work in a Fortune 500 company, by the way, or a megachurch, that might sound eerily familiar! The centurion's job is to follow orders and keep his roughly eighty men in line.[1]

Like my dad, this centurion had a dirty, thankless job. Nobody expected greatness from him. Nobody wasted time wondering why he hadn't achieved "greatness." *He* probably didn't even waste time wondering that. Instead, he focused on keeping his eighty guys in line, following orders, and probably sending incredibly boring reports to his superior officer. And when a crisis came, and the life of his servant was hanging in the balance, he simply took the next step, and then the next.

I'm going to let you read the full story for yourself, because the actual plot isn't where I want us to focus. Rather, I want to highlight how the story ends: with Jesus marveling

---

[1] Hang on, I know what you're thinking: "He had *one hundred* men, you dope . . . he was a *centurion*." That's what I thought too, until my research team—i.e., *Wikipedia*—informed me it was more like eighty. (And don't tell me you don't consider *Wikipedia* an authority on first-century Roman military protocol!)

in verse 9, "I tell you, I have not found such great faith even in Israel."

I love that. Jesus chooses *this* guy to hold up as an example of faithfulness. A foreign soldier who showed up every day and went to work.

This is a good time to be absolutely clear. I'm definitely not knocking the *possibility* of moving from good to great. Sometimes greatness happens, and frankly, it's awesome. Take a business in my neck of the woods: Story Coffee. It's a pop-up coffee bar, and I'm not jerking your chain when I tell you that the owner makes the best macchiato I have ever tasted outside Italy. It's fair to say that in a world of poor, average, and good coffee, Story Coffee is great.

Does that mean every coffee shop everywhere in the world needs to strive to become great? Nope. Sometimes you need a coffee that's too fast to be great. Sometimes you need a coffee that's a third of the price. In fact, Story Coffee might not exist anymore by the time you read this.

Greatness comes in moments. Like lightning. But my fear is that too many of us leaders think *everything* needs to move from good to great. And that's simply a lie.

Not every dinner you cook for your family needs to be a gourmet feast. Sometimes—most times—it just needs to be healthy, filling, and tasty and bring you together as a family.

Not every board meeting you run needs to be as shareable as a TED Talk. Sometimes—most times—it just needs to move efficiently through the agenda.

Not every shut-in you visit as a pastor needs to hug you,

teary-eyed, as you leave. Sometimes—most times—they just need a friendly face to disrupt their boredom.

But our culture has such a hard time with stuff like this. There's an entire *industry* of so-called gurus who prey on our feelings of inadequacy. We might be good leaders, or effective leaders, or respected and liked leaders . . . but are we *great* leaders? Wait, maybe we're not! And surely we ought to be! We're leaders in the greatest nation on God's green earth, and if *we're* not great every single moment, who will be?![2]

This message gets sprayed around like a sneeze during flu season, by leagues of salespeople and marketers and social-media types and authors chasing a quick buck. And the only thing they're *really* selling is a puffed-up feeling of importance.

Remember that briefcase full of sunglasses? The centurion would have loved that. If he broke a pair while sparring with one of his legionnaires, he'd just reach into his satchel, pull out the next identical pair, and get busy with his next job. As my dad would say, perhaps grabbing his hundredth pair of sunglasses, "Just get the job done."

Let's start to define success as competency. I'm willing to bet that what your organization or church truly needs tomorrow is mundane. A budget report filed. A conversation with someone. Two dozen e-mails sent. I know that's true for my business almost every single day.

So let's show up and get it done. Let's clock in tomorrow and choose to be good before being great.

---

[2] Have you noticed that I can be a little sarcastic sometimes?

If you've got a problem with that, you can go buy your own fancy pair of sunglasses.

LESSONS FROM THE JUNKYARD

If everything is great, nothing is great. Great is relative.

Most of the world, most of the time, runs on competency, *not greatness.*

We should strive for greatness when appropriate. But most of the time, getting the job done is good enough.

Let's clock in tomorrow and choose to be good before being great.

16

MANAGEMENT TECHNIQUES ARE ADDICTIVE

Leadership techniques and tricks work . . . until they don't.

The first time it was my job to lead a staff every day, I was all of twenty-three. The material from my management courses was fresh in my memory. I had dog-eared textbooks and high-lighted notebooks filled with axioms, laws, and flow charts. I had popular books by all the business gurus of the day.

However, my results were far from perfect—which, as we know, is business-speak for "pretty bad."

Basically, nothing I tried was effective in motivating my staff. Sure, some of what I tried worked some of the time—but I always felt like I needed *more*. A new technique. An insightful thought experiment. A fresh way to pitch things to my employees. And as soon as that grew old, it was back to my supply of management techniques. I could never seem to locate the magic technique that would solve all of our issues.

Turns out, I simply needed time, perspective, and experience in order to realize there *is* no magic technique, even though leaders are constantly being sold the promise of one. Years passed, and as I dumbed my way into actually leading—rather than reading and talking about leading—I learned a second vital truth.

Management techniques are addictive.

The problems we face in our organizations are very real, so it's natural to search for answers. Because we want answers so badly, we're predisposed to believe whoever is selling them . . . and we can never get enough.

We've all seen blog and book titles like "Five Fast Ways to Tune Up Your Team" or "Why Saying No Helps You Say Yes." But if we're going to be that obtuse, how about "Staff Management Tips from Pro Wrestling" or "How to Use Jargon to Confuse Your Team and Consolidate Your Leadership."[1] Point is, we could read those blogs and books forever and never be satisfied—and our teams would *still* have issues.

We're basically talking about narcotics in the form of hardcover books. The periodic rush of gambling via weekly leadership e-mails. And like any addictive substance, the effectiveness of any management technique decays over time. The second or fifth time you apply Gary Guru's

---

[1] We could even start a blog called *Junkyard Wisdom*.

Patented S.T.A.F.F. Technique (Smile with Teeth, Always Face Forward) at a meeting, your coworkers stop thinking you value their input and start getting creeped out.

Over time, colleagues and employees begin to get wise to the tricks you're using. Heck, *you* begin to get wise to the tricks you're using! So you need *another* dose of fresh ideas, then another, then another.

There's even a spiritual-industrial complex—yes, it's a real thing—that gets church leaders hooked on how to build large, growth-oriented churches. Hire an entertaining pastor (tattoos are a bonus) and a worship band that sounds (and looks) like Coldplay, buy at least one fog machine and three espresso machines, and always have *tons* of parking. Make sure you have an airy, modern, and well-appointed worship center. And most important, go to multiple conferences and retreats each year in order to keep up with the latest and greatest techniques. And don't worry . . . it's all for the sake of growing God's Kingdom.

Know what? People *will* show up—for a time.

But the techniques that draw people are both fleeting and addictive. If a church grows by one thousand people its first two years, the leadership can come to *expect* that growth to continue, no matter that it's unsustainable. (The same thing happens in business.) So the leadership is constantly tempted to improve, tweak, innovate, change, scale, revamp, and so on.

I'll be honest: It took me too many years to figure out the real problem.

The problem isn't any particular techniques I'm using or missing, and it's certainly not my people.

The problem is my motivation. Whether I'm conscious of it or not, far too often, I manage people in order to achieve a self-serving end. If I can get my employees to perform better, my organization's bottom line will grow *and* I'll gain recognition for being the leader who orchestrated it.

But if I remove that selfish motivation, would I *really* read another book by the latest management guru? Probably not. Certainly not as often. It would help me focus my attention on the few management lessons that speak specifically to my situation, rather than being distracted by bestseller lists and insider jargon.

The antithesis of caring about the management tricks is to care about people. The best managers put their people first, period.

That sounds easy, but it's exceedingly difficult. There will always be other motivations competing for priority. Many of those competing motivations are vital, by the way, such as profitability, sustainability, and so on. But the best bosses and managers are those who truly care about the people they lead. That's incredibly hard yet incredibly important.

If you get it right—caring about and serving your team— you'll be able to read management books less often and more effectively *because you're reading for the right reason.*

If you get it wrong, well, maybe my next book will be just the twelve-step program you need.

SALVAGED FROM SCRIPTURE

In Matthew 14, we read about how Jesus feeds a basket-ball arena full of people.[2] The disciples watch in amazement, but apparently, they don't learn very much. We know that because one chapter later, Matthew tells us that Jesus feeds yet another basketball arena full of people. Same desire on the part of Jesus, same failure on the part of the disciples. He gives them every opportunity to step up to the challenge, but even after the first unbelievable feeding, the disciples insist on pointing out the logical impossibilities of what Jesus is asking.

Obviously, these were extraordinary events, so I don't want to push this analogy too far, but if Jesus had been a certain sort of modern management guru, thinking more about techniques than people, there might have been a *very* different result!

After the first miracle, Jesus would have created met-rics and documented exactly what he did, so the disciples would have a template for the future. Then, when the sec-ond opportunity arose, he would have scolded the disciples for forgetting the lesson, shouted something about getting with the program, and reminded everybody, "We've been over this, people!"

But he didn't. Instead, he responded out of compassion for both the hungry people *and* the disciples. Rather than

---

2 "The number of those who ate was about five thousand men, besides women and children" (Matthew 14:21). That's like your neighbor asking, "How many should we expect for dinner?" "Just one," you reply, "besides my wife and three kids." Sheesh. Anyway, a basketball arena = five thousand men + five thousand women + some happy kids.

referencing previous methodologies or chastising the disciples, Jesus stepped up and served like a loving leader.[3]

The disciples lacked faith, not knowledge or experience. They kept coming up with technical reasons not to lead—money, scale, distance to town—but Jesus saw it differently. He didn't see a management technique that was being poorly implemented. He saw people who needed compassion, patience, and love.

LESSONS FROM THE JUNKYARD

Because we want answers so badly, we're predisposed to believe whoever is selling them.

The best managers put their people first, period.

---

[3] Jesus *did* sometimes chasten the disciples, but it tended to be about things like ultimate truth. When hungry or hurt people were in front of him, he typically focused on their health before anything else.

17

BABIES DON'T EARN PAYCHECKS

*Dysfunction must be addressed clearly
and quickly in the best interests of others.*

Can you imagine one hundred acres of broken-down cars? That's an area the size of about forty Walmart stores. That would be a lot of concrete flooring filled with everyday low prices . . . except these acres were covered with wrecked cars and the overpowering presence of grease, oil, mud, dirt, grime, and, yes, rats.

To my father, it was heaven. It was the biggest junkyard in the business, and he couldn't resist the chance to buy it. Of course, it meant he had to move to the Central Valley, away from his home of fifty-plus years in the Bay Area, but that was a small price to pay for junkyard nirvana.

I'd only been out of college a few years when Dad moved.

We had been running Goble Properties together for a few years, and Dad had already built or purchased multiple properties, some of which he built on land that was previously used for the junkyards. The company had blossomed as the demand for commercial real estate space boomed in Silicon Valley. He left me behind in San Jose, which meant I had to step up and manage the industrial and commercial properties. It was trial by fire for a twenty-four-year-old, but it was also a once-in-a-lifetime opportunity, so I tried to do my best.

At the time, we had eight guys doing building maintenance for us. We operated on a never-ending treadmill of tasks: light fixtures that needed replacing, doors that wouldn't lock or unlock, adding a small office for a new tenant, graffiti removal, and so on. Many of the guys were former junkyard employees, so they'd known me for years. Still, since I was younger than all of them, they viewed me as a "college boy" with little real authority.

It took some time to establish myself as the leader, but what I did wasn't particularly difficult. Arriving to work early, lending a hand on dirty jobs, or just buying beer went a long way. Making clear that some of the complex jobs they had to do were not beyond my understanding helped a lot. And, of course, my signature was on their paychecks—the ultimate authority.

Soon, daily operations were smooth enough that I started to relax a bit. I was getting the hang of managing the crew.

Famous last words . . . because that was when the

maintenance guys decided to star in a low-budget soap opera, written and produced by them.

For reasons that were never clear to me, seven of the eight guys began arguing. (The eighth guy couldn't be bothered to care one way or another.) They weren't bantering, either. Their verbal fights quickly escalated to a choosing-alliances-on-a-reality-show level. Guys came to work angry, requested to work less with certain coworkers, and took their gossiping to a depressingly new low. All that dysfunction was like acid eating away at their job performance. Job assignments were completed only halfway, or even skipped.

When the bickering had first started, it had all seemed so silly and pointless that I shook my head and ignored it. Oops. Because one morning, two guys refused to drive to work on a big project together. I frantically reshuffled the job assignments for the day, hoping to juggle schedules and personnel and still get our current punch list completed. I failed, and my makeshift crews failed. That month, we didn't have our planned tenant improvements completed on time, which meant a tenant couldn't move in on time, which meant we lost rent.

I was fuming. I kicked myself for not putting the kibosh on the drama early on, but I'd assumed the issue would go away on its own. I hadn't wanted to waste my leadership capital on such a minor issue. But now I had a nasty problem that would only get worse. There wasn't time for team building or conflict resolution. I couldn't afford to have a listening session with each worker. What I needed was a crew who could put a fresh coat of paint on a commercial warehouse, not sing "Kumbaya" together.

I thought about it overnight and finally came to the conclusion that being direct with these guys was always best. So the next morning, I pulled them together in the shop before they went out on their jobs.

"The second worst part of my job is firing people. I really hate doing that because somebody loses their livelihood, which harms their family."

Safe to say, I had everyone's attention after that opening!

I continued by saying, "Firing somebody is only the *second* worst part of my job, though. You know what the first is? Changing your diapers! I refuse to have people around who act like infants, constantly crying and whining and complaining that the other guy doesn't share toys. I won't change your diapers—not now, not ever—so if I'm faced with a choice of firing you or changing your diapers, you *will* be fired. Now get back to work."[1]

That was it. No discussion of the issues, no airing of hurt feelings, no opportunity to process.

And you know what? It worked. In fact, it worked beautifully. Some of the guys smiled when I said it, and all of them recognized how silly they had been.

Well, almost all of them. One of them was just too stubborn, and within a couple of weeks he quit—proving that babies don't earn paychecks. But the rest of the crew? Their respect for me went up, job performance went up, and job

---

[1] There may have been a few other words in that rant, as well.

satisfaction went up. Not only was this true in the short term, but decades later, I stay in touch with many of them as they enjoy their retirements.

SALVAGED FROM SCRIPTURE

We can see a similar dynamic of dysfunction in Mark 10:35-45. Two of the disciples, James and John, decide to shoot for the moon. They get Jesus alone and tell him, "We want you to do for us whatever we ask."

(Direct quote. Let that sink in for a second.)

Jesus, being perfect and all that, responds flexibly. "What do you want me to do for you?"

The brothers ask if they can sit *really close* to Jesus in heaven, one on the left and one on the right. (As a brother, I can guarantee they had privately "agreed on" who would get the left and who would get the right.)

Wouldn't you know it, word gets back to the other ten disciples, and they are *not* pleased with James and John trying an end run. They become indignant. Dysfunction is infecting the group, and Jesus—unlike me all those years ago—puts an immediate stop to it. He calls the Twelve together and says, in verses 42-45, that the way of the world is to jockey for favor and respect. Once you get it, according to the world, you've earned the right to lord it over everyone below you. "Not so with you," Jesus counters. "Instead, whoever wants to become great among you must be your servant, and whoever wants to be first must be slave of all. For even the Son of Man did not come to be served, but to serve, and to give his life as a ransom for many."

Dysfunction can't be allowed to fester.

Even a small amount of dysfunction can gradually break down a team—and I guarantee your team has better things to do than bicker about who gets to sit by Jimmy on the way to a maintenance call or who gets to sit by Jesus on the way to heaven!

LESSONS FROM THE JUNKYARD

Firing somebody is only the second *worst part of my job, though. You know what the first is? Changing your diapers!*

Even a small amount of dysfunction can gradually break down a team.

SECTION THREE

LEARNING IS ONE THING,
BUT WISDOM? THAT TAKES A
BIT MORE TIME AND REFLECTION.

18
SCALE LIKE AN INVESTOR (IF YOU WANT TO MESS UP YOUR LIFE)

Never ever think you have to "scale up" to be successful.

Recently, a business friend invited me to an evening event.[1] I declined because of an unbreakable previous commitment: dinner at home with D'Aun. He was surprised by my refusal to attend, and with complete sincerity, he asked a version of this: "You've been married for what, thirty years? How in the world does your wife still want you home for dinner? I don't get it."

"It's simple," I answered flippantly. "I don't hang around with people who are obsessed with scalability."

Probably because my answer made very little sense outside

---

[1] Signs you might be one of my "business friends": You regularly use words like *impact, disruption, bleeding edge,* and *core competency*. You know who you are.

my own head, my friend asked for an explanation. Here's a version of what I told him.

Investors worry about scalability. Why? Because their primary concern is generating returns.

There are certainly nuances to this I won't go into here, but a reasonable summary is that most investors are in it for the short term, whereas most business owners are in it for the long term. An investor is more or less an ATM, except the kind of ATM that expects to be paid back with interest. A business *owner*, however, can operate within a different set of values and a different definition of success.

And that puts scalability in a whole different light.

When investors push the idea of scalability, what they're really after is an increase in returns. Owning ten pizza restaurants is cheaper than owning one, on a per-restaurant basis. And owning a thousand is even cheaper! But what about the owner of all those pizza restaurants? There are quite a few things money can't buy, and one of them is being able to be present with your family on a regular, relaxed basis.

This is why a wise business owner pushes down roots before branching out. "This is my corner pizzeria," our imaginary and wise business owner says, "and I am now an integral part of this community."

Would that owner be thrilled to someday have fifty pizza joints? Five hundred? Likely! (But not necessarily, and not automatically.) First, however, that owner needs to be rooted in the community. Go deep before going wide.

Maybe you don't own a business. Maybe you have no

intention of ever owning one. Still, the principle remains. No matter what we focus our personal and professional energy on, setting the goal of *bigger bigger bigger* is a recipe for burn-out and even failure—and harms other people in our lives, as well.

Shortsighted leadership prioritizes "impact" over relationships, while long-term leadership does the opposite. Entrepreneurs can be especially vulnerable to the temptation to go wide before they have roots. They say they want to change the world . . . but don't know their neighbors. They push to be the first to market . . . but can't find the time to volunteer at their kids' events. Slowly but surely, they fall in love with their vocations . . . while married to their spouses. They are the type of people, as I wrote in my first book, who lock their car doors driving through a bad neighborhood on the way to the airport . . . and then fly to a developing country to do a service project in a bad neighborhood. They fall for the big vision, the grand scheme, but overlook the neighbor next door.

As leaders, it isn't always a literal investor we attempt to satisfy. Sometimes our own expectations or assumptions are what burden us. Sometimes our personal ambitions create more havoc than any outside pressures.

Want to know one reason why my wife (and family) still likes having me around? Because I never became *inordinately* enamored with scale. I never chased it only for the sake of getting bigger. I worked—pay attention to the fact that this is a concrete, intentional verb—I *worked* at keeping the values of my company the same as the values of my family. My business grew, yes, but organically, like a tree's roots enable it to spread its branches.

Together, as a family, we embraced community, honesty, and balance. Yes, I mess this up sometimes. Okay, lots of times. So does my company. But my aim has been consistent through the years, and I pray it's true, as well.

So even as my family gives me high marks—and still likes hanging out with me—investors would likely label me a "low performer." Their gauge for success is what I *could* have done with my business if scaling up was the only thing I cared about.

Good thing it isn't!

Effective leaders create a metric for "success" that aligns with their personal and family values. I've worked hard to be able to focus on the parts of my life that truly matter. Like having dinner with my wife or texting my daughter during the day. Like having a beer with my son or attending my Bible-study group.

Simple, good, nonbusiness activities—whether spending time with family or coaching a local sports team—are a much better way to scale. Running a business with deep roots and being an engaged, relational citizen are the true measures of business success.

SALVAGED FROM SCRIPTURE

The story of Joseph is told, in fits and starts, between Genesis 37 and 50. He starts out as the favored son. The younger kid who gets spoiled by Dad. He's got a fancy coat and seems to have ambitious plans to scale into a leader to be reckoned with. He has even fancier dreams—and of course he decides it's a good idea to tell his older brothers they're going to bow down to him.

What a guy . . . he probably reminds my siblings of me! Favored, ambitious, annoying.[2]

Fast-forward many chapters and many years and Joseph's brothers are indeed bowing down to him. However, the route that takes him there is full of treachery and pain and regret.

God used Joseph to do something good for his family, and for that matter, all of Egypt and many surrounding nations. It sure was a wild ride getting there, however, and it had little to do with Joseph intentionally scaling. Rather, Joseph had to go deep, relying on God, rather than on political connections or social status. Then when *God* did the eventual scaling, it shocked Joseph, along with everyone else!

LESSONS FROM THE JUNKYARD

A wise business owner pushes down roots before branching out.

Shortsighted leadership prioritizes "impact" over relationships, while long-term leadership does the opposite.

Effective leaders create a metric for "success" that aligns with their personal and family values.

---

[2] To be fair, most of us with siblings would describe each other with at least two of those three words. Doesn't mean we don't love each other, just that we're siblings.

19

BORING IS GOOD

*Innovation is sometimes necessary, but tried and true effort—
the boring stuff—is what gets things done.*

A while back, a friend told me about a grant that might be perfect for one of the nonprofits I lead.

"You've got a great shot at this, Roy," he urged, "and it's six figures. It's worth trying, right?"

How could I object? Our nonprofit dutifully filled out countless forms, submitted documents, and calculated all manner of data—even really obscure stuff only a foundation's grant officer would dream of asking for. The process took plenty of time. So much time, in fact, that we lost some of our focus. Submitting the application meant we did less of the good work our nonprofit was supposed to be doing. We knew that's how the game is played, though, so we did our best to play nice. We told ourselves it would be worth it if the grant came through.

Several weeks later, we learned the foundation had awarded the grant to another nonprofit. I was disappointed but not upset. That sort of thing happens. But then I read further about why another organization received the grant. The other nonprofit was—and I'm quoting the award announcement here—"cutting edge" with a "scalable" model that "better leveraged resources" to "maximize the impact."

Good grief. I'll take Foundation Clichés for $1,000, Alex.

Obviously, I was disappointed we didn't get the grant. And obviously, the foundation had the right to distribute money as it saw fit. But I wish foundations—and, yes, churches— were a bit more grounded in their thinking.[1]

Funding innovative projects *can* be great. We need creative solutions to be field-tested, and sometimes a novel approach is what solves an intractable problem. I'm grateful Jonas Salk developed a vaccine against polio, for example, despite being out of the scientific mainstream of his day. And who knew Khan Academy[2] would be so transformative and, yes, innovative?

Most of the time, however, we ought to invest in tried and true systems that already work. For every unprecedented, out-of-the-box idea that succeeds, there are ten established, trusted ideas *already* succeeding.

The problem, of course, is that tried and true systems

---

[1] A pastor recently asked me how his church can "maximize outcomes" with their missions budget, what "innovative" steps my nonprofit is working on, and how we can "quantify" the impact their support makes. Sigh. The church is just as guilty of this as most foundations.

[2] A nonprofit educational organization that hosts thousands of online tools to help students around the world succeed.

are *boring*, and it's really hard to get donors and volunteers excited about boring. Foundations often want sexy, and understandably so, if they want their annual reports to be cool and compelling. But if they want to change the world, more often than not, they should settle for sweat pants rather than sexy.

Which reminds me of myself—not the sweat pants, but the boring. Most days, most of my time, I do boring stuff. Real estate rentals, farming, teaching, mentoring. These are good things, but they are boring in a culture that wants everything to be new and exotic all the time.

I'm not drilling wells for blind orphans who were once child soldiers, or inventing a new app that will improve your love life, fill your bank account, and shine your shoes. But the boring stuff I'm doing is making a difference. It might not be exciting to a PR agent, but it's good. My company rents affordable space to small businesses, and our ministry PathLight provides sponsorships for at-risk students. My daughter's nonprofit works on *prevention* of child exploitation, not the glamorous kicking-down-doors-to-rescue-girls stuff. These are solid, productive projects that actually make our world better.

Prevention is boring. Funding education is boring. Lease agreements are boring. *But these things are exactly the things that deserve our support.*

Am I saying we ought to support programs and organizations *because* they are boring? Actually—yes!

If they are well executed and proven to have an impact,

then boring organizations *need* our help in a big way! Think about it: In a world of shouted pleas for support, the folks doing boring work are the ones who have the hardest time getting any attention. They need our support.

What this ought to mean for leaders is a renewed focus on the good, the necessary, and, yes, the boring. Let's forget about the sexy and the cool for at least five minutes. It reminds me of a pastor and author I know who recently learned an article of his would be featured in a magazine. The publisher asked for a photo, so naturally, this pastor sent a picture of himself sitting in a coffee shop, reading a book, decked out in his hip twentysomething shirt, and bending his arm *just* enough to make his tattoo visible.

Naturally that annoyed me! Do I want him to send in a lousy picture instead? Of course not. Do I have a point here? Not really. Except most of us should probably use photos where we're behind the wheel of an SUV as we drink lukewarm coffee from a fast-food cup while on the speakerphone with the dry cleaner. Not so cool, but much more real.[3]

It's the same with our leadership. We probably don't need to be flashy tomorrow . . . but we certainly need to be faithful.

SALVAGED FROM SCRIPTURE

Even readers of Scripture can fall prey to this temptation to choose sexy over steady. Take Paul, the outspoken, combative

---

[3] Full disclosure: I am massively uncool and perfectly content with that. Now my collaborative writer, David, must be pretty cool because he spends all his time in coffee shops. I wonder if he has a hip twentysomething shirt and a tattoo?

leader. How many books and sermons and arguments has Paul generated?

But consider Paul's sidekick, Barnabas. He doesn't show up all that often in the New Testament. We don't know much of what he said or wrote or thought. We don't argue about his theology because, well, we don't really know what it was! He wasn't flashy or controversial. Truth be told, Barnabas was boring. He seems to have been a loving and affirming guy, yes, but also boring. A scriptural afterthought.

Yet his contemporaries in the early church loved him, admired him, and were thankful to God for him. I suspect that without Barnabas traveling alongside Paul and encouraging him, Paul's cross-Mediterranean missionary journeys would have looked much different, or perhaps failed altogether. Barnabas was boring, and sometimes boring isn't just good—it's essential.

LESSONS FROM THE JUNKYARD

We probably don't need to be flashy tomorrow . . . but we certainly need to be faithful.

Sometimes boring isn't just good—it's essential.

20

PERFECT PEOPLE MAKE LOUSY LEADERS

If you try to lead by being perfect, you will disappoint yourself and those who rely on you.

When I was sixteen, my friends assumed I was good at fixing cars. It seemed reasonable. I'd been around cars for most of my life. But what my friends failed to consider was that in the wrecking yard, the valued skill wasn't fixing cars but *dismantling* them. Fixing was what our customers did.

So I could rip parts *out* of a car pretty well . . . and then I could stare at the pile of parts and wonder how to put everything back together! Like the time I was seventeen and bought a dilapidated Datsun pickup at a car auction. I drove it home and immediately started stripping out the interior. I had no real plan, but I knew the interior was ugly, so it needed to go if I wanted to look cool driving it.[1] Uncle George (of radio-smashing infamy) happened to stop by when I was in the middle of my project. "Typical Goble," he commented. "He gets a new car and immediately starts to tear it apart."

Turned out, he was right. I never did finish the interior. And the next summer, I drove that pickup with a buddy all the way to Alaska with the seats unbolted to the floor. Which was great when we stopped at campgrounds; we were the only ones for miles with comfortable seats to use by the campfire! Stupid, yes, but unforgettable.

The point here is that leaders need to be willing to jump in and attempt to figure things out, even if that results in failure. Trying only the things we can't fail at is a recipe for mediocrity.

That lesson was part of my dad's business DNA. Dad never allowed perfection to get in the way of productivity at the junkyard. Back then, if you wanted to get things done, you needed to get grease on your hands and figure it out. There was no such thing as a project that stalled because no one "knew how to do it." If we knew how, we did it—and if we didn't know how, we learned as we went. It didn't matter if no one knew how to remove a Mercedes transmission without destroying it . . . someone simply learned by doing, or else broke it into a million pieces. Either way, perfection was never allowed to get in the way of productivity.

One year, employees from the various junkyards in the

---

[1] And, despite writing earlier about the value of being boring, and despite the truck being an ugly old Datsun, I *did* want to look cool driving it.

area got together for a giant picnic. We had all the elements of a great afternoon at the park: savory carne asada smoking on barbecues, engines revving as guys arrived, bags of potato chips, and beer. Lots of beer.

To make it more fun for everyone, there were games. Not piñatas or sack races, but games for wrecking-yard guys. In one, competitors raced to get a piece of window glass out of a door—and the glass had to be perfectly intact. In the first round, one of our guys who I'll call "Jose" came in second. We were shocked, since Jose could take *anything* off a car in about thirty seconds flat. His competitor, though, had taken advantage of a gray area in the rules: He simply shredded the interior panel of the door so he could get to the glass faster. Jose took the panel off carefully, as he would have done in Dad's yard, since it could have been resold.

Still, Jose's second-place finish was enough to earn him a trip to the final round. Next time, he absolutely *obliterated* his door panel and then removed the glass, winning in a landslide. It wasn't perfect—that interior door panel was in tatters—but it was fast and effective. It got the job done.

There's another reason why perfect leaders will disappoint: Trying to be perfect is exhausting. Perfection is slow, obviously, and that can be okay *sometimes*. I absolutely want my future cardiologist to take her time and get each detail exactly right. But for every heart surgery that needs to be perfect, there are countless everyday tasks and situations in which attempting to be perfect is incredibly draining. Perfectionistic leaders will burn out, disappointing everybody who relies on them . . . and followers are likely to burn out even faster as they try to keep pace.

So back off the accelerator a little bit. It's okay if you don't earn that A-plus every single time.

Remember, perfect leaders are often exhausted and get far less done than leaders who can learn from others—and their own imperfections.

SALVAGED FROM SCRIPTURE

So am I contradicting the Bible here? Jesus tells us to be perfect—"Be perfect, therefore, as your heavenly Father is perfect" (Matthew 5:48)—and Goble tells us not to worry about being perfect.

Maybe. I'm always open to the possibility that I don't have my head on straight.

But think about this. A few chapters later in Matthew, we see the rich young ruler meeting Jesus. The guy is pretty confident he's done all the right things. All the *perfect* things, like keeping the law and whatnot. But Jesus sees the imperfections in what *looks* like a perfect life from the outside. And because he is a loving leader, Jesus challenges the young man with direct honesty.

"If you want to be perfect, go, sell your possessions and give to the poor, and you will have treasure in heaven. Then come, follow me" (Matthew 19:21).

The man walks away in sorrow, and Jesus turns to his disciples and remarks, "Truly I tell you, it is hard for someone who is rich to enter the kingdom of heaven. Again I tell you, it is easier for a camel to go through the eye of a needle than for someone who is rich to enter the kingdom of God" (verses 23-24).

The disciples are floored. Wait, this guy was rich *and* he was perfect! If he can't get into heaven, who can? And a camel through the eye of a needle—seriously?!

They turn to Jesus and say, basically, "So you're telling us that *no one* can be saved, right?"

Jesus answers them: "With man this is impossible, but with God all things are possible" (verse 26).

This is the key. We aren't going to save ourselves. We *can't* save ourselves. We can't be perfect leaders, just like we can't put the parts back together on an old Datsun pickup.

But can God? Now the story changes. Suddenly, we realize our own imperfections mean we should walk with humility. We know we are not as good as we want others to think we are, and so we become deeply thankful for grace. Yes, Jesus calls us to live lives of perfection—but Jesus also points out that's not even possible!

We need God to help and lead us. And with God leading, we become far better suited to lead others. Want to be a good leader? Give up on perfection and focus more on God. Not only will you be a better leader, you might even figure out how to put a Datsun pickup interior back together.

LESSONS FROM THE JUNKYARD

Trying only the things we can't fail at is a recipe for mediocrity.

Perfectionistic leaders will burn out, disappointing everybody who relies on them . . . and followers are likely to burn out even faster as they try to keep pace.

We need God to help and lead us. And with God leading, we become far better suited to lead others. Want to be a good leader? Give up on perfection and focus more on God.

21
QUESTIONS FOR YOUNG (AND DUMB) LEADERS

Too often, we try to influence the next generation with lofty principles and complex management techniques when what is really needed are simple questions that force young leaders to evaluate both their performance and their objectives.

God, in his infinite wisdom and grace, gives us multiple warning signs that we are growing old. Our children leave home for college, for example, or we begin to grow weirdly long ear hair.

There's another sign too: Young leaders start asking if you will mentor them. It seems like once a month or so, another sharp, young leader asks if I would be willing to serve as a mentor.[1]

Despite my crusty reputation, I say *yes* a surprising amount of the time. I know what it's like to want a mentor—and

---

[1] Or if they're beating around the bush, they say something like "Could we like maybe hang out sometime and talk about stuff?" Millennials, man.

need a mentor—but not be able to find one. I never benefited from that relationship as a young man in my twenties and thirties. (I know what you're thinking. *Did you actually ask anyone?* Yes. Quite a few people, in fact, all of whom said *no*, which tells you something about what I was like back then.)

My father mentored me, of course, from when I partnered with him right after college until he passed twenty-five years later. He profoundly influenced the course of my life. And in some ways, my older brother mentored me as well. But family is different. Having a mentor who doesn't share your DNA is extremely valuable. A good mentor can size you up in a way you never can yourself.

So I'll agree to mentor a young leader, and usually it's a great deal of fun. We'll meet for great coffee, take a walk in the hills, or grab a beer. Last month, I even had a hatchet-throwing contest with one of my mentees! Occasionally, the conversation can be unpleasant, and sometimes it's a nuisance in my schedule, but the joy of mentoring far outweighs any negative experiences.

Part of that stems from the five mentoring rules I follow. They set the tone before our first meeting, which stops a lot of problems before they start.

1. Don't lie to me or I'll destroy you.
2. Take my advice, give a good explanation for why you aren't, or stop wasting my time.
3. Be vulnerable about what you really need help with

and come prepared with thoughtful questions and reflective answers . . . or at least bring a bottle of good wine.

4. Don't miss one of our appointments unless someone dies.[2]

5. I can ask you anything. There are no "off-limits" questions. Deal with it.

The basic idea behind all these rules is that neither person can hide behind evasions or nonsense, and that both people will engage with tough questions and hard answers. That means mentees can take seriously *anything* the mentor says, good or bad, because they trust the mentor has their best interests—which in this context means "growth as a leader"—at heart.

SALVAGED FROM SCRIPTURE

We can see this dynamic in action within a single chapter of Matthew's Gospel.

Jesus is mentoring Peter, and since Peter is a hothead, he needs a bit of everything from Jesus. So Jesus is talking to Peter in Matthew 16, and he tells Peter how blessed he is . . . oh, and by the way, Peter is going to be the foundation of the church, and Jesus is giving him the keys to heaven. That's some serious affirmation! And the simple question for Peter becomes *Are you ready?*

---

[2] Cats and other pets don't count. I'm talking only about family members—and dogs, obviously.

It's not too long after, however, that Jesus rebukes Peter, telling Peter he's interfering with Jesus' mission . . . oh, and by the way, he compares him to literally the worst thing in the universe, which is Satan. And the simple question for Peter becomes *Whose side are you on here?*

That's what mentors do. They give you affirmation and they give you grief—and good mentees take both seriously.

Jesus was the greatest teacher and leader in large part because he wasn't afraid to ask tough, practical questions to dumb, young leaders.

How about us? Are we willing to mentor? If so, are we willing to ask exceedingly simple—and serious—questions?

LESSONS FROM THE JUNKYARD

A good mentor can size you up in a way you never can yourself.

Jesus was the greatest teacher and leader in large part because he wasn't afraid to ask tough, practical questions to dumb, young leaders.

22
SILOS

Sometimes silos—independent divisions or people in your organization—are exactly what you should create and protect.

The thing about golf is that unless you're really good, you should probably stop after the first nine holes. Things always get a little squirrely after you've been playing too long.

My problem is I'm not very good or very smart—and I'm stubborn—so I keep going. My game gets worse and worse, but I've found that the conversation often gets better and better. After wasting two strokes in a sand trap on the fourteenth hole, people are so sick of the stupid game that they're willing to talk about *anything* other than golf.

Even organizational silos![1]

"Everyone hates silos these days," I said, hoping the two

---

[1] By the way, I work a lot in Belize, where there are hundreds of islands and atolls, but almost no actual silos. So if you find yourself in Belize and need to explain this concept, refer to *islands*, not silos.

pastors I was playing with were as sick of golf as I was. "It's all team-leadership-this and organizational-integration-that. Everyone hates it when the right hand doesn't know what the left hand is doing, right?"

"Right," agreed one, "and I assume there's a 'but' coming?"

"*But* everyone who hates silos is missing the point. Sometimes silos are really nice! I actually think we need more silos these days."

One of them sighed so audibly I could hear it from the other side of the fairway. "Ignore him," he shouted to the other pastor. "He's always saying things like that just to get a rise out of us."

Okay, so that might be true. But it's missing the point. I really do think silos are underappreciated.

We all know about the bad things silos can cause. When organizations create sealed-off, independent departments—silos—those departments tend to think only of their own responsibilities. As a result, they do little to help other parts of the organization. It can become every department for itself, even if that means the organization as a whole suffers. Thus, silos are being torn down at a breakneck pace as leaders strive to prevent this kind of myopic and potentially harmful thinking.

However, like most handy leadership principles,[2] *destroying silos is only a good idea until it isn't.*

It turns out that silos can be quite nice! They can be appropriate, useful, and wise. The fact that some silos are bad doesn't lead to the conclusion that all silos are bad.

---

[2] Including the ones in this book—don't forget.

It's like when I was growing up in the junkyard. Dad made very sure *I* stayed inside a silo!

Obviously, he didn't want me using an acetylene torch at the age of six. Neither did he want me listening to the yard guys discussing their sex lives. Those were occupational hazards of working in the junkyard for the workers, but he wanted to protect me as long as he could.

On the other hand, Dad also needed to protect the junk-yard from me! He knew I could screw things up really fast. I might break a valuable part in my haste to take it off a car, or I might—hypothetically—drive the yard truck into a pole. (I *still* claim the steering broke, though I was hard-pressed at the time to explain why the steering worked just fine after the accident.)

So my junkyard silo was the right leadership decision. Slogging through a series of menial (but relatively safe) jobs kept me contained, even as I matured. I clambered in and around the racks holding our countless used tires, for example, using my bright-yellow paint marker to indicate tire sizes. Or I searched through a massive pile of individual hubcaps, looking for matches I could wire together and hang on a display wall.

Those were jobs no one else would do. They kept me busy, taught me to work, and contributed, even in a small way, to the family business.

That same wisdom applies to a lot more than kids in a junk-yard. I admire well-run organizations that staff departments or programs with good people paying attention to a common, useful goal, even if those teams are internally focused. The key word is *focus*. Silos are great at keeping teams and individuals concentrated on a specific task or project. The walls of such a silo define expectations, provide opportunities for direct feedback, and encourage shared accountability. There is less unproductive conversation in a silo, and employees are asked to attend fewer meetings that waste time. In short, silos can encourage more clarity and more productivity.

That can be *exactly* what a leader needs.

Let me be crystal clear: Silos aren't always good. They can limit growth, for example, and organizations that cooperate across organizational lines often exhibit fresh energy and creativity. My positive opinion about silos doesn't describe organizations with a domineering or tyrannical leader or ferocious look-out-for-number-one cultures. Those situations are not to be admired.

But here's a funny thing about silos: If we change the word to *boundaries*, suddenly everybody loves them! Yes, there *is* a difference between the two, but it's a subtle difference. Smart leaders need to recognize that sometimes silos have real value. Don't discount them in general without evaluating their specific role in your organization.

SALVAGED FROM SCRIPTURE

Paul used to be Saul, and when Paul was Saul he was one mean man. His idea of a fun afternoon was watching a Christian or two get crushed to death by stones. So after Saul met Jesus on the road to Damascus and radically rethought his life choices, the Christian church in Jerusalem was skeptical, to say the least. Saul—now Paul—suggested, "Hey, let's preach the gospel together!" And the church's response was "Yeah . . . no."

Still, the church couldn't discount the possibility that Paul was transformed. They had to take a chance on him. High risk, yes, but *very* high reward. He was a talented, charismatic leader. So the church sent Paul away for something resembling a gap year (or three, or more) to let him figure out who he was in Christ and how he would minister. (And also to make sure he wasn't still crazy and/or homicidal.)

The Jerusalem church basically put Paul in a silo, allowing him to travel across the Mediterranean and refine his message and theology. He did his thing while Peter and the Jerusalem church did their thing. Paul grew to understand the gospel in a fresh, more Gentile-centric way because he'd left the confines of Jerusalem. Eventually, Paul and Peter came back together. There were hard words, arguments, and reconciliation . . . but you can read about that on your own.[3]

The point is that the first-century world was turned upside down, in a good way, by this silo approach . . . and we are beneficiaries two thousand years later.

LESSON FROM THE JUNKYARD

The fact that some silos are bad doesn't lead to the conclusion that all silos are bad.

---

[3] Arguing about traveling companions, or who to dine with, was complicated in the societal structure of the first century. Barnabas and Paul disagreed about John Mark in Acts 15 (verses 36-41), and Peter and Paul disagreed about who to eat with. Was there reconciliation? Probably. Peter alludes to this in 2 Peter 3:14-16 and Paul in Galatians 2:11-19.

23
RISK-ADJUSTMENT SCHOOL

Our risk aversion makes us do silly things to "stay safe"—and it keeps us from doing important things that aren't safe.

I'm feeling cranky about risk.

We've gone *way* too far with all the protections we've tried to add to our lives. We want to be safe. We *need* our kids to be safe. We idolize safety—and we've redefined the word to mean *the prevention of any negative experience.*

Consider this for more than a millisecond and its absurdity is revealed. Such so-called safety is impossible, of course. It's not possible physically, mentally, emotionally, or any other way. We break arms playing sports. A professor challenges our assumptions. Couples break up. Bosses yell at us. Coworkers annoy us. Then there's the really nasty stuff we can't control, like wildfires and cancer and war.

Life isn't safe, and it never will be. Pretending otherwise is a lie. The ultimate example? Safe sex . . . are there any other two words more contradictory?

Recently, I gave a short talk and shared a funny junkyard story. It's way too unsafe for this book—yes, I see the irony— but it was about not being wimps, rolling up our sleeves, getting grease on our hands, and tackling challenges.[1] It was about taking risks, how trying to remain "safe" is a fool's errand, and how the pursuit of false safety actually *prevents* us from doing certain types of good.

Afterward, during the Q&A, one of the guys in the audience asked a question.

"Roy, I like what you're saying about risk . . . can you give some specific ideas for how I can safely break the wealth bubble my kids live in?"

Snort. (I snorted mentally, of course. I'm not usually *that* rude.) He got what I was saying, and he wanted to get his kids out of their bubble and allow more risk in their lives, *but he wanted to do it safely*. That's like wanting to learn to swim without getting wet.

When I turned sixteen and got my license, I drove with a buddy from San Jose to Arizona. We had no seat belts, no cell phone, no credit cards, and no real plan. Halfway there, we stopped for the night at a roadside hotel. We spent several days with our friend in Arizona and drove home. I didn't call my folks once. No news is good news, right?

---

[1] Nope. I can't even tell you in the footnote. Maybe if we're having a glass of wine together sometime, and my publisher doesn't know about it.

Put your hand up if you'd allow your sixteen-year-old to do that. Put your hand up if you're an adult and you *still* wouldn't consider doing that!

Here's the deal. Safety is overrated. It isn't pointless, of course. Seat belts save lives. Preventing factories from dumping carcinogens into rivers is a good thing. However, when we fixate on safety—on supposedly preventing any negative experience—we do lasting harm. We passionately desire to feel alive because we've lived lives of bubble-wrapped sterility.

Here's a great example from the church. I've had people give me the following *real, actual* excuses for *not* taking their kids—and themselves—on a short-term trip to a developing nation to learn and serve. They might be frightened. They might get severe jet lag and have their sleep schedule interrupted. They might be bitten by a bug or catch a virus. They might suffer a severe sunburn.

Know what? They might. You might. But do it anyway!

We need schools specializing in risk, uncertainty, and occasional peril. Not usually literal schools, of course, but opportunities that will teach us how, when, where, and why to *build relationships with people who are different from us*. Life will be less about *safe* spaces and more about *good* spaces. Overvaluing safety will always apply the brakes to our service and commitment. If safety becomes a driving force—or even exists as a constant echo in the back of our minds—then we will never quite dream enough, never go far enough, never risk enough to do all we can for those God loves.[2]

---

[2] This is true in our churches, too, by the way!

If you want to be a leader, you better know how to embrace risk. Cultivating an environment where risk is a normal part of your daily curriculum will challenge you and your team. Some will grow tired and maybe even quit. You will be stretched in ways you hadn't considered. But you'll advance through the school of learning and grow in your competencies to handle risk.

Look, if you're in leadership, by default, you are not in a safe position.

But doesn't it feel good to risk in order to gain? Leaders do this all day, and really great leaders thrive on the joy it brings them. This isn't the high a compulsive gambler gets with each roll of the dice, but there *is* a bit of that in our passion to lead. Even a reluctant leader—which I've been from time to time—finds great satisfaction in taking a risk for the right reasons.

What matters most is Kingdom risk. In our businesses, our churches, our families, Kingdom risk is what will bring Kingdom reward. We will discover—and be part of creating—goodness, transformation, and love. Upon graduation from risk-adjustment school, we will have learned to live by faith, not fear.

Here's the simplest way I can say it. Stop worshiping safety (or "Safety"!) and start worshiping God. Heed the command to love your neighbors. Amazing things will happen, I guarantee it. Not safe, but amazing. And deeply, life-changingly good.

We want to have it all, but we can't. Break the bubble

or be safe—choose one. And remember that if you choose "safe," you can't guarantee that, either.

SALVAGED FROM SCRIPTURE

Most of us are familiar with the most Jesus-y talking lion in history: Aslan. In C. S. Lewis's Narnia books, Aslan is a kind of stand-in for Jesus, or at least what Jesus might be like if he were walking and talking with the people of Narnia, rather than earth. In *The Lion, the Witch and the Wardrobe*, Mr. Beaver offers this unsettling commentary on Aslan.

> "Safe?" said Mr. Beaver; "don't you hear what Mrs. Beaver tells you? Who said anything about safe? 'Course he isn't safe. But he's good. He's the King, I tell you."[3]

Ironically, picturing Aslan as not-safe-but-good is *safer* than picturing Jesus that way. In the Narnia books, it is the characters who risk everything to follow Aslan. Our danger as readers is merely vicarious.

The real Jesus, however, is explicit about the risk of following him. Read the plain words of Jesus in the Gospels. If we follow him, we will be persecuted. Families will be split apart. We may be called upon to give up our very lives. We will have trouble—that's a promise from Jesus!

Sounds like a dark cloud with no silver lining.

---

[3] C. S. Lewis, *The Lion, the Witch and the Wardrobe* (New York: HarperTrophy, 2000), 80.

But that's another one of those tensions at the heart of the gospel. In John 16:33, after warning his disciples about some of these very risks, Jesus says, "I have told you these things, so that in me you may have peace. In this world you will have trouble. But take heart! I have overcome the world."

Peace is different from safety. The God we follow never promises safety, but he absolutely promises a peace that passes understanding. That's exactly what we need to remember as we face up to risk.

LESSONS FROM THE JUNKYARD

Life isn't safe, and it never will be. Pretending otherwise is a lie.

If safety becomes a driving force—or even exists as a constant echo in the back of our minds—then we will never quite dream enough, never go far enough, never risk enough to do all we can for those God loves.

If you're in leadership, by default, you are not in a safe position.

24

LEADERSHIP AS A CODE WORD FOR *POWER*

Leadership *becomes a code word for* power *anytime we equate good leadership with having loyal followers.*

The cult of leadership has run amok.

This struck me several years ago when I was sitting next to a good friend at a conference. She was a keynote speaker, which meant she and I were sitting in the front row of a large convention center. The conference organizer, a good man who has years of experience in his field, had just been introduced and was being applauded.

At that moment, my friend leaned toward me and whispered, "He likes being on the stage just a *little* too much."

Now, you might view this as a snarky thing to say, especially about our host. And in some ways, it was! But in another way, my friend was exactly right. I knew the organizer well, and he was definitely a good guy, but it was true

145

that he craved the spotlight more than he should. It got me thinking about leaders who *led* essentially by the act of being a well-known leader. There was an echo-chamber effect. Celebrity leaders are famous for their leadership, which can tempt them—sometimes cause them—to fall more in love with fame and attention than with actually leading.

Later in the conference, I attended a breakout session where the same guy taught about the fundamentals of leadership. It was a reasonably good session, though not particularly thought-provoking. Later that day, I was thinking through some of the key points he had made, and it struck me how easily each instance of the word *leadership* in his talk could have been replaced by the word *power*.

That's when it really hit me: Many confuse leadership with power.

These leaders see the opportunity to be a celebrity leader—the one on the stage, the one getting the applause—as an opportunity to build power and influence.

If you are a leader at *any* level, the evidence is abundant. Keynotes and commencement addresses give certain people a platform to polish their own credentials as they inspire (or bore) the "next generation of leaders." Authors spoon-feed us acronyms and numbers that magically add up to effective leadership. Seminars claim to unleash the leader within. Thought innovators package their tweets and truisms, hoping to hit it big with the next big leadership book.[1]

---

[1] Ouch. Guilty.

However—and I'm saying it again to emphasize this point—many leaders equate *leadership* with *power*, and there are serious consequences to this.

See, many of us have an understandable desire to "take it to the next level." Who wouldn't want to improve? Yet that makes many of us—and our organizations—all too eager to bow down to kiss the feet (and sometimes the rear end) of the latest, greatest leader. We want what they've got. And that's a big, big problem.[2]

Focusing on leadership isn't harmful in and of itself. The issue is when leadership becomes the *only* thing we focus on. Good leadership is worth celebrating, yes. Of *course* it is. However—and this distinction is vital—even *good* leadership is never worth worshiping. After all, good leadership can help organizations and people flourish and grow. That's what we're in this for. As a culture, however, we've long since blown past the line between celebrating and celebrity worship.

Put simply, our society fetishizes powerful leaders. Since we desire that same admiration, we cloak our pursuit of power with the language of leadership. Too often, leadership is lifted up at the expense of other valuable organizational and personal values like wisdom, love, joy, transformation, patience, and service.

In reality, leading means serving. Leading often means setting down power, voluntarily. It's difficult, usually thankless, and definitely not for the lazy. Any of us can be tempted

---

[2] So big that I'm writing a two-part lesson about it. In a later chapter, I share more about leadership and power as it relates to the church.

to pursue power and disguise it as leadership, which is why all of us need to seek accountability and practice humility.

SALVAGED FROM SCRIPTURE

Here's a great story about a lust for power disguised as "leadership," starring two of our favorite disciples, James and John.

> As the time approached for him to be taken up to heaven, Jesus resolutely set out for Jerusalem. And he sent messengers on ahead, who went into a Samaritan village to get things ready for him; but the people there did not welcome him, because he was heading for Jerusalem. When the disciples James and John saw this, they asked, "Lord, do you want us to call fire down from heaven to destroy them?" But Jesus turned and rebuked them. Then he and his disciples went to another village.
>
> LUKE 9:51-56

Insane. It's like if you're taking a walk with your kids and you whistle to a dog that's sitting on the sidewalk ahead of you. Instead of approaching you for a nice scratch, however, it runs away. To which one of your kids responds, "Want me to go punch that puppy in the face a few times?"

What?! No! *But Jesus turned and rebuked them . . .* what I wouldn't give to have a recording of *that.* He's resolutely walking toward his own death, and his disciples—who he's been mentoring for three years, by the way—want to napalm a village just because they couldn't stay there overnight.

Scripture is full of leaders who used their leadership positions to amass personal power. Confusing the two is a temptation we all face. Disciples, pastors, junkyard operators . . . it's a never-ending battle to keep our best instincts to serve from being corrupted into a grab for power.

LESSONS FROM THE JUNKYARD

Many of us confuse leadership with power.

Focusing on leadership isn't harmful in and of itself. The issue is when leadership becomes the only *thing we focus on.*

25
GET OFF YOUR PEDESTAL BEFORE IT GETS KNOCKED OVER

Leaders must lead themselves before blindly accepting the leadership of others.

In the previous chapter, I suggested that our culture's fixation on leadership is often a fixation on power, but this junkyard story reminds me that what we usually consider "power" isn't always needed for effective leadership.

There were two key positions in the junkyard: the front-counter employees who interacted with customers and sold parts and those who worked in the yard organizing the wrecked cars and pulling parts. Most of the power resided at the front counter. That's the first place a customer engaged with us, it was where the money was collected, and it was where the smarter guys worked (or at least the more socially presentable guys).

Now, guys working on the front counter could be real jerks to the guys in the yard. It wouldn't last long—they'd be shown the door by the boss, or the guys in the yard would make their lives miserable. But it did happen from time to time. They let the relative power go to their heads.

And then there was Roberto, a longtime employee of my dad. When a customer ordered a part over the phone, Roberto would head into the yard and make sure the pullers got exactly the right part in the right condition. He was always competent, never bossy. Everyone in the yard loved working with him because he got a ton of work done with no drama—and he had fun along the way.

Quiet, unassuming, and utterly reliable, Roberto was a model leader. I fondly remember him whistling throughout the day, usually some Mexican song I'd never heard. He showed up to work a few minutes early each morning and never shed his dirty overalls until the last customer had left and the front gate was locked. His diligent, under-the-radar work was essential to keeping the yard working smoothly.

Every person who worked for Roberto regarded him highly. He *was* a leader because the people who worked with Roberto listened to him, respected him, and admired him.

Fifty years later, I expect those who were fortunate enough to work with Roberto still remember him. I know I do. He was a man of strong character, a faithful Catholic who loved his family and his job. In fact, Roberto was an *ideal employee* for my dad—and I use that wording intentionally to show how easy it is to slip into our false paradigm of power and leadership. Did you catch yourself thinking anything similar to *But he was* only *an employee?*

It's time to swing the leadership pendulum away from celebrity leaders and toward Roberto. Here are some ideas about how we can get there.

First, the obvious: Character is paramount. As an old business mentor of mine said, "Hire for character because competency can be taught." A leader who is not doing everything possible to build character is one who will eventually fail.[1] Leaders with character resist being put on a pedestal rather than climb over others to get there.

Second, leadership is about accessibility. As technology and leadership merge, we expect leaders to be available . . . or at least *potentially* available. My friend Bob Goff is a master of this, publishing his personal phone number in the back of his bestselling book *Everybody, Always.* He answers every call himself! Tell him Roy referred you, and marvel at his accessibility. I'm not quite as brave as Bob, but you can reach me whenever you want at roy@junkyardwisdom.com.

Third, my final idea is more of a hope. Somehow, individually and collectively, we need to disarm the system of overvaluing leadership. This means that as followers (and we are all followers), we must stop putting good leaders on false pedestals. How? By honestly identifying a leader's strengths *and* weaknesses. Scary, yes, and countercultural, but doing so is an act of love.

---

[1] My friend and colleague Gayle Beebe wrote about this in his book *The Shaping of an Effective Leader: Eight Formative Principles of Leadership* (Downers Grove, IL: IVP Books, 2011).

Let's encourage leaders to embrace vulnerability and affirm them when they are vulnerable. Let's celebrate humility.

SALVAGED FROM SCRIPTURE

The Bible is never afraid to speak truth to power. From the Psalms to the Old Testament prophets to Paul, holding the complacent to account is an integral part of God's interaction with humanity.

Jesus did the same. And to get the mood of the verses we're going to look at here, it helps to picture Jesus in a particular way. You know that Sunday-school painting where blond Jesus is holding a lamb and looking into the distance like a stoned high schooler in a senior portrait? That's *not quite* the Jesus in action in Matthew 23.

Instead, imagine that Jesus getting shot up with an overdose of adrenaline, ripping the head off the lamb he's holding, and massaging the blood into his beard and his golden locks until he looks like a psychotic (but still perfect) MMA fighter.[2]

That's a more accurate image for the Jesus who lobs this verbal grenade:

> Woe to you, teachers of the law and Pharisees, you hypocrites! You shut the door of the kingdom of heaven in people's faces. You yourselves do not enter, nor will you let those enter who are trying to. . . .

---

[2] If you're listening to this on audiobook, oops—sorry if the kids were in the car!

You snakes! You brood of vipers! How will you
escape being condemned to hell? Therefore I am
sending you prophets and sages and teachers. Some
of them you will kill and crucify; others you will
flog in your synagogues and pursue from town to
town. And so upon you will come all the righteous
blood that has been shed on earth, from the blood
of righteous Abel to the blood of Zechariah son of
Berekiah, whom you murdered between the temple
and the altar. Truly I tell you, all this will come on
this generation.

MATTHEW 23:13, 33-36

Yikes. The teachers of the law and Pharisees were a bunch
of power-hungry religious bigots trying to cloak themselves
as mere servant leaders. And Jesus tore that cloak right off
their backs so he could whip them with it.

Double yikes . . . I'm a Christian leader as well.

And the alternative Jesus offered? It's in Philippians 2:1-18,
but that's a Scripture for another book.

LESSONS FROM THE JUNKYARD

Hire for character because competency can be taught.

*Encourage leaders to embrace vulnerability and affirm them when
they are vulnerable. Celebrate humility.*

26

IS IT LONELY AT THE TOP?

It's only lonely at the top if you get there the wrong way.

At this stage of life—successful enough to fool people into thinking I'm wise, wise enough to know success is fleeting, and old enough to have thought deeply about all of this—young leaders regularly ask me deep questions. Recently, I was meeting with a mentee over sandwiches. Just as I crammed a huge bite into my mouth, he asked, "Would you say it's true that it's lonely at the top?"

"That all depends," I managed as I chewed, "on how you *get* to the top."[1]

A lot of folks define leadership as an individual endeavor.

---

[1] By the way, the question presupposes that there is a *top* a leader can get to. I'm not so sure there is. Healthy leaders never feel they have made it to the top . . . and always see Christ at the top.

One person with a vision rallies and directs others to achieve that vision. It's easy to see how such a leader, upon reaching "the top," might be lonely. Others define leadership more collaboratively. In this model, a leader works within the context of a team to build vision, generate consensus, and move forward. Even in this model, a leader can feel isolated at the top. At the end of the day, collaboration has trouble crossing levels on an organizational chart—and friendship even more so.

When people ask me which model is best, I always tell them it depends. Context is everything. Team leadership tends to move more slowly but go farther, while a talented individual can race off the starting line much more quickly. There are many variables, of course. A family business obviously makes decisions—and chooses a leader or leaders—in a different way than corporate structures. Small churches can offer more community, but also tend to put more on the shoulders of a single leader. Sports teams, medical staffs, construction crews . . . there are differing models best suited to each situation and personality.

Generally, I lean toward an individual model when organizational goals are well-defined and relatively modest. My dad ran his junkyard this way, and it worked well for him. He didn't need buy-in or collaboration from the colorful employees . . . he just needed them to take cars apart without setting too many things on fire or starting too many fights. On the other hand, I lean toward a collaborative model when organizational goals require buy-in from more than a few people. A company that wants to go public, for example, needs all the internal consensus it can get. Same goes for a church—and one advantage of team leadership is that any single leader can step away from the organization and the organization will keep ticking along.

I've seen success with both models, depending on how you define success.

I've also seen clear weaknesses in both models, *possibly* because both rely on human leadership!

What unites these ways of leading, however—and what I want to focus on in the context of my mentee's question—is the potential for a friendless leader, at the height of power yet regretting a lack of human connection. If you're a die-hard individualist in your personal life, then you will absolutely be lonely at the top, regardless of your leadership style. If you value collaborating at work and operate within a team, you are much less likely to be lonely—but it's not impossible!

No matter how your organization functions, value people as people. Listen. Don't run roughshod over others. Avoid being a jerk unless it's absolutely necessary. How you get to the top will largely determine how much you enjoy being there. Lead the right way, all along the way, and loneliness will be one thing you don't need to worry about.

SALVAGED FROM SCRIPTURE

I love Nehemiah, in part because he's a fellow builder. In the biblical story, the Israelite Nehemiah is living in Persia but working as a powerful government official. When he hears that Jerusalem's walls have fallen into disrepair, he secures permission to return to the ruined city and repair it. What follows is a master class in leadership. Nehemiah is the guy with the vision and charisma—a classic go-it-alone type— except he secures incredible buy-in from the other Israelites. Soon, the entire city is helping to rebuild the wall,[2] and less than eight weeks later, a massive project that probably should have taken a year is finished.

The result is a nation with more than rebuilt walls—its pride and self-identity have been rebuilt as well. Nehemiah is viewed as a sacrificial leader, and at the same time, he personally benefits from his place within a renewed, united community.

On the other hand, the Bible is full of lonely leaders. To pick one example out of many, think about Samson the judge. He wanted to be known as a powerful leader—and he was— but he scared or offended so many people it was always a one-man show. Eventually, he was brought down from leadership and humiliated, at least in part because he had refused to build wise and strong relationships in his rise to power.[3]

LESSONS FROM THE JUNKYARD

No matter how your organization functions, value people as people.

How you get to the top will largely determine how much you enjoy being there.

---

[2] The way Nehemiah accomplishes this is refreshing and relevant. Check out Nehemiah 1–7 for further reading.

[3] See Judges 13–16.

SECTION FOUR

WITH WISDOM COMES RESPONSIBILITY
TO KNOW YOURSELF, ACCEPT FAILURE, AND ACT—
BUT YOU SHOULD STILL DRINK GOOD CHAMPAGNE.

27
YOUR BUSINESS WILL FAIL (GET OVER IT)

Sometimes it takes more faith to walk away from the things we have started than it takes to start them.

There's a business adage that nine out of every ten businesses fail.

Nonsense.

Ten out of every ten fail! It's simply a matter of time.

This isn't a philosophical point. It's *literal.* Literally all businesses fail at some point. Many fail fast, some last for decades, and a rare few last past the century mark. But at the end of the day—or the millennium—they all fail.

And with rare exceptions, nonprofits and ministries follow the same trends—and live by the same delusions—as businesses. All organizations eventually fade out of existence, cease operations, or morph into something altogether different. No organization lasts forever. Yet the adage makes it seem as if a good leader ought to move heaven and earth in order to be the *one* business out of ten that "doesn't" fail. By this metric, ninety percent of organizations are led by failures, while ten percent are able to rise to the top and survive.

Again, nonsense. One hundred percent of organizations fail.

Instead, a good leader will ask, "When will it fail?" and "How will it fail?"

In 1986, D'Aun and I rode a snowmobile to inspect a remote property in the Sierra. (More about this to come.) The cabin on that property became Hidden Lakes Retreat, which in turn became the launching point for dozens of other endeavors, including similar facilities in places like Brazil, Zimbabwe, and Belize. Those in turn set in motion even more endeavors, like a college-chapter program launched from the Jaguar Creek property in Belize, as well as a "save the rainforest" program. Other spin-offs included an academic program, a national magazine, and hundreds of short-term service trips around the world.

Why am I bringing up these old stories? Because a lot of people have a hard time walking away from a dream—myself included. Years later, when it was time to step away, we found it was difficult. Part of our identity was tied up with the organization we'd poured so much of ourselves into.

But walking away was the right choice. We worried about language at the time—resignation, retirement, transition—but honestly, we quit. With some good reason, of course. We were exhausted and out of ideas. We were hoping new leadership could infuse the organization with new energy. Sadly, several years after our departure, parts of the organization eventually died, or at least went into a coma. It became a statistic . . . since ten out of every ten organizations fail.

My real estate company works with hundreds of small businesses. Over the years, I've seen many leaders pour everything they have into a failing venture, hoping desperately to save it . . . only to lose it anyway.

They would have been better off walking away sooner. The smart thing to do in many situations is to simply pull the plug on an organization rather than let it drift along in a state of decay. Free up those resources so they can go to work elsewhere. This doesn't mean we should simply shrug and give up on an organization. If there is vision, purpose, and energy for the organization, then keep working. But we need to balance the hoped-for wind behind the sails with the real possibility that we're simply adrift and about to die of dysentery.[1]

I've been there. I've helped launch churches, small businesses, and nonprofits. I know that gut-level feeling of not wanting to turn your back on a vision. *How could it be in anybody's interest for me to quit now? We've come so far, and our work is so important. I can't let people down.*

---

[1] Frustrated by the seemingly vague, perhaps contradictory nature of this advice? Want clear, unambiguous answers? Want a program to follow? Then do not, under any circumstances, read my first book, *Junkyard Wisdom*.

Those are challenging questions that seldom have clear answers. But I can tell you this: When we stepped away from our vision, we put more effort into making it a healthy transition than we ever put into starting the organization in the first place! That's why it usually takes more faith to leave an organization than to start one.

Part of the trouble is our tendency to assume—not always correctly—that every charity and nonprofit and parachurch organization "does good" and "makes the world better" in some way. When one of those organizations fails, then, our assumption is that less good will be done in the world.

That, of course, is mostly nonsense. No organization is perfect, and new organizations continue to rise up even as others fail.

Getting over our fear of failure will allow us to do important things. Sometimes a leadership change, or even a change in mission, means an organization can pursue a new vision that brings life and vitality. Sometimes an organization needs to shut down completely. Sometimes we need to lock the doors and walk away. This can allow change in ways that wouldn't be possible with us still around.

Often it's something in between . . . isn't the tension great?

As leaders, then, let's try to take fear of failure off the table. We *will* fail. We might even fail spectacularly—like flames and screaming and weeping and everything! That's okay too.

Whatever happens, though, you as a leader are going to need faith.

SALVAGED FROM SCRIPTURE

I love how Peter fails his way into succeeding. There are so many examples of him bungling things, but think about this classic:

> Now Peter was sitting out in the courtyard, and a servant girl came to him. "You also were with Jesus of Galilee," she said. But he denied it before them all. "I don't know what you're talking about," he said. Then he went out to the gateway, where another servant girl saw him and said to the people there, "This fellow was with Jesus of Nazareth." He denied it again, with an oath: "I don't know the man!" After a little while, those standing there went up to Peter and said, "Surely you are one of them; your accent gives you away." Then he began to call down curses, and he swore to them, "I don't know the man!" Immediately a rooster crowed. Then Peter remembered the word Jesus had spoken: "Before the rooster crows, you will disown me three times." And he went outside and wept bitterly.
>
> MATTHEW 26:69-75

Why does he weep bitterly? Partly because Jesus is right next door, getting the tar kicked out of him by a mob of angry pastors. But more because earlier that same night, Peter had *sworn* that even if he had to die with Jesus, he would never disown him.

Life comes at you fast sometimes.

But as we know, Peter's failure didn't preclude Peter's success in following Jesus! The Holy Spirit continued to work through him, Jesus continued to reveal himself to him, and miracles continued to happen through his work.

In fact, Scripture is full of people who fail—often in spectacular style—and end up serving God. King David, of course. Jonah and Abraham. Jacob, Zechariah, Samson, the disciples . . . you get the idea.

God can use our failures. Actually, God *has* to use our failures, *because all of us will fail.* Just as our organizations will eventually fail, we will too. If our conception of serving God is tied up with being perfect, and remaining perfect, our hearts will remain stunted.

LESSONS FROM THE JUNKYARD

It usually takes more faith to leave an organization than to start one.

Try to take fear of failure off the table.

God can use our failures. Actually, God has to use our failures, because all of us will fail.

28

KNOW THYSELF

*Your success as a leader depends
on knowing who you really are.*

My wife, D'Aun, is English by ancestry. She's a whole bunch of other things too, like Dutch and German, but generally speaking, she's English.

Me though? I'm like *English*. Picture cod fried in beef drippings and piping-hot chips, flavored with salt and vinegar and wrapped in newspaper. That's how English I am. I have a DNA test showing thousands of years of tea-sipping existence on a few small islands off the European continent, with five hundred years of documented English genealogy.[1]

Once, when D'Aun and I were in London for a visit to

---

[1] Nearly four hundred of them here in America.

the Tower of London and a beautiful display commemorating the fallen of World War I, we found ourselves wading through a thick crowd of people, all of whom seemed to be making progress past us while we went nowhere. We were trapped on a treadmill of strangers' faces.

Suddenly D'Aun stopped, looked at me, and said, "You can really tell we're in England."

She paused the perfect amount—just long enough for me to *start* to ask the inevitable follow-up question—and then she cut me off.

"A lot of pale skin and big noses."

I laughed out loud as I responded, "My people!"[2]

My skin is so pale I need sunscreen under a bright moon, and my nose *is* kinda big—though I insist it is still proportional to my head. I can't dance. Or sing well. I was a mediocre athlete and merely an above-average student. I can't cook and I'm often too sarcastic (duh). The only thing that comes easy in my leadership—sometimes too easy—is bossing people around.

A vital part of leading well is understanding yourself and then embracing the way God made you. Not the way you *wish* you were, but the way you *are*. Sure, we can learn new things and modify our habits, but some fundamental aspects of ourselves will never change . . . and that's a good thing!

Who am I? I'm a white male real estate developer who

---

[2] If you just started to think, *But Roy, don't you know that England, and London especially, are incredibly diverse now?* please stop. I know. D'Aun was talking about my ancestry, not current demographic trends, and we were surrounded by countless people who could have been my great-great-great whatever.

follows Jesus . . . and far too often, I'm ashamed of how white people have treated people of color, how men have treated women, how real estate developers have valued short-term profits over long-term community, and how people of faith have too often embraced expediency over faithfulness.

But I also know that my unique mix of traits, my unique mix of experiences, all the things that make me, well, *me* are still valuable. My voice matters. It might be blind to certain perspectives, it might only be one voice in a culture that needs many more, but it still matters.

And here's the thing: Your voice matters too.

Look, this isn't some sort of pep talk where we hold hands and sing together at the end. Frankly, I'm sure we could spend some time together and I could find a lot of things we'd disagree about—and vice versa! We'd have a great time arguing. But we need to own who we are. That doesn't mean we sit idly and *remain* who we are. After all, God is constantly working on us. But it means we embrace who we are, warts and all, and (here's one of those leadership tensions) humbly yet confidently be ourselves.

As Socrates so wisely put the matter, "You do you."

Wait. That was the Internet who put it that way—Socrates said something closer to "The unexamined life is not worth living," which was probably based on the Greek aphorism "Know thyself."

But the point remains the same. Own up to who you are—and who you aren't—as a person and a leader. Be prepared to humble yourself—especially if, like me, you have the privileged position of being part of a majority in your culture. Be prepared to listen a lot, and be prepared to shut up sometimes. Knowing who you are is *not* a license to run roughshod over others. Don't be a jerk under the guise of "being yourself."

Instead, recognize both the value *and* the blind spots you bring to the organization, the culture, the situation . . . and proceed from that point of self-knowledge.

If you do, people will be thankful for your authenticity.

And if you don't? Everyone will know you're a phony.

SALVAGED FROM SCRIPTURE

Here's an amazing story about knowing who you are as a leader. In Judges 4, we read about Deborah, a prophet and "judge" (or leader) of Israel. One day, she summons a warrior named Barak to appear before her and says, basically, "You're going to take ten thousand troops and slaughter King Jabin's forces, which are commanded by Sisera and backed up by his nine hundred super-chariots. Got it?"

Barak isn't so sure of Deborah's prophetic ability or judgment (heh), so he tries to hedge his bets. After all, going up against super-chariots—even at ten-to-one odds—isn't a recipe for a long life.

"Sounds like a plan," he tells Deborah, "as long as you go with me."

Why does he ask this? It's a setup. If he fails, she'll share in the blame, and if he succeeds, he figures he'll get the credit, since he's the warrior and she's just the judge. Or maybe he's a coward, has no faith, or is a wimp.

While Barak is playing checkers, however, Deborah is playing chess. She surprises him by immediately agreeing, then surprises him even more by shaming him. "If I go with you, all the glory for taking down Sisera will be mine. We *will* take down our enemy, but the headline will be that a woman beat him, not your army."

The battle goes exactly the way Deborah predicted. Barak's troops rout Sisera's men, and Sisera abandons his soldiers and flees on foot, hoping to live to fight another day. He ends up in the tent of a woman named Jael, who encourages him to rest . . . and then when he falls asleep, she takes a hammer and drives a tent peg through his temple and into the ground. Talk about one tough woman![3]

The next chapter in the book of Judges tells us there was peace for more than a generation.

Deborah knew who she was: a prophet who had been given a clear vision of God's plan, a strategist unsurpassed in her generation, and a woman. *And* she knew her limitations in the eyes of the people around her: no military experience (that we know of), no storehouse of riches to buy results, and being a woman in a patriarchal society that tended to demean her gender. She didn't shy away from leadership, and she didn't shy away from being a woman, even though she knew

---

[3] Isn't the Old Testament amazing? Ask your preacher to cover this text! And remind me to tell you about the time a car door chopped off part of my wife's finger, and she picked it up and drove herself to the hospital. Women are awesome.

the two often weren't compatible in that culture. The result was good for everyone . . . except Jabin and Sisera, of course.

LESSONS FROM THE JUNKYARD

A vital part of leading well is understanding yourself and then embracing the way God made you. Not the way you wish you were, but the way you are.

Own up to who you are—and who you aren't—as a person and a leader.

29
THE FREESTARTER™

"Lead, follow, or get out of the way"—
but what about going your own way?

Lead, follow, or get out of the way. It's a clever line that we often quote in our leadership culture, and there is a fair amount of truth to it. If you're not out front leading your followers, you'd better be a team player and try to keep up . . . otherwise, you don't belong in the game.

As with most leadership principles, however, the truth is more complex. Sometimes we find ourselves in a situation where choosing between traditional "leading" and "following" isn't possible[1]—but fortunately, getting out of the way is *not* our only option!

---
[1] A decision that is more often than not out of our control.

SALVAGED

Here's an example. As I mentioned in chapter 27, D'Aun and I founded a tiny faith-based, environmentally friendly retreat center that accidentally, over the course of fifteen years, expanded to twenty-seven countries. It began in one country, of course, inside a small cabin in the Sierra, way back in 1986.

To understand how unlikely our journey from shoestring to global was, it helps to picture the cultural mood at that time. I was a white male real estate developer with a degree from a Christian college and no international experience to speak of.[2] Guys like me were supposed to turn a cold shoulder to environmentalists. Environmentalists were, in the thinking of the time, the godless liberals who cared more about trees than people, while we were the godly ones who cared more about souls than cyanide pollution.

Except when D'Aun and I were seniors in college, we attended a study program in the Sierra. Between snow camping, rock climbing, and cross-country skiing, we did course work on a crazy new area of theological study: biblical creation care.

The course convinced me to rethink my perspective. If God had created, well, *creation*—and called it good— shouldn't we do the same? Shouldn't we care about what God cared about, especially because the poor are the ones who suffer most when we *don't* care for creation? On the drive home, I turned to D'Aun and asked, "You know, someday when we're retired, wouldn't it be cool to start our own little

_____
[2] Today, those things are a mix of still true, sorta true, and less true.

retreat center and host small groups and talk to them about creation care?"

All I was thinking was a little cabin in the woods when we retired. God had different plans, and on a much faster time line. We ended up chasing that dream long before we retired. Rather than waiting forty-five years until our retirement, God led us to launch the retreat center just five years later.

And then the wild ride really got going. As our organization grew by leaps and bounds, we found ourselves facing a long list of tasks. We were supposed to mobilize volunteers, organize and lead creation-care projects, build environmentally sustainable conference centers, found on-campus chapters of the organization, equip and mentor campus leaders, communicate with donors, create curriculum, speak with churches, and on and on and on.

We weren't afraid of hard work, and we cared passionately about the issue . . . but there was a major roadblock: *Nobody* else was doing what we were doing. Nobody had even tried. Sure, there were a few books about creation care written by scholars, and a few think tanks trying to influence theology. But no organization was actually trying to *practice* creation care.

Lead, follow, or get out of the way? Those early years we weren't really leading by most cultural standards set for leadership. Hardly anyone showed up—and many who did came only because of the gorgeous location or the low prices we offered!

Were we following then? Nope. We were on our own, making it up as we went—and, sadly, disagreeing with the leadership of most churches along the way!

So, did we get out of the way? Not by a long shot. In fact, we were very much *in the way* of a lot of people! If you're younger than about thirty-five, you may find it strange to hear that pastors and church leaders were *not* fans of creation care. And no matter what age you are, you won't be surprised to hear that secular environmentalists don't tend to be cheerleaders for the church. A friend, Peggy Campolo, told D'Aun and me something as profound as it was unsettling. She said we were building a bridge between the church and environmental groups—and bridges are meant to be walked on.

Ouch.

Going your own way can be painful. Looking back, though, our decision to go our own way helped to create a movement that incrementally but surely changed the church. Today, outside of a handful of extreme churches, you would be hard-pressed to find a pastor advocating rapacious or even "merely" careless behavior toward the environment. Creation care is rightfully orthodoxy (sound doctrine) for twenty-first-century Western Christians, though we still have a long way to go in terms of practice.

You might say we became leaders as our efforts gained traction. Okay, I'll grant you that. But in the beginning, we were visionaries, prophets, crazies, outliers . . . choose your definition. But not leaders.

This story isn't unique. We all know someone or about someone who had a "crazy" idea that is now accepted and even imitated. Who are these crazy people? I've found there are three types.

The prophet. A prophet doesn't always have followers, but neither does a prophet follow an earthly leader. Prophets are often on the margins of society, or entirely outside it. The Old Testament is *full* of prophets who operated on their own, rejected by both the powerful and the powerless. But prophets, by definition, don't "get out of the way." Quite the opposite: They stand *in* the way, often as a solitary witness or warning.

The artist. "Getting out of the way" seems like the natural state of being for many artists. How else to describe a solitary printmaker or playwright, working alone late into the night? Yet the art produced, if it is genuine art, cannot "get out of the way." Art has the creative and spiritual power to disrupt, shape, and influence the world. Artists, like prophets, see things from a different viewpoint than the rest of us. In the words of Emily Dickinson, they "tell it slant,"[3] helping us to understand God, our world, our neighbors, and ourselves in new and transformative ways.

The Freestarter™. I had to make up a term to describe this last type of "go your own way" leader. A freestarter carries a mix of the zeal of an entrepreneur, the creativity of an artist, and the vision of a prophet. When we launched our retreat center in the Sierra, we were freestarters.

---

3 Emily Dickinson, *The Complete Poems of Emily Dickinson* (London: Little, Brown, 1976), 506.

Here's a simplistic illustration. Say a group of people are wandering down a country road in the English countryside, lost and confused. At last, they reach an intersection. A leader might say, "Let's go this way." A collaborative leader might say, "Let's spend a few moments as a group figuring out which way to go." Either way, if the leader is operating out of her strengths, the followers are happy to follow because they sense wisdom in the leadership (or because they are fearful to do anything else). A few people might "get out of the way," simply stopping where they are and waiting for help.

A freestarter, however, engages in the decision-making process, listens to the ideas about how to proceed, and then, finding none of the options palatable . . . leaves the road and cuts through the adjacent field. Nobody follows. Most think the freestarter is crazy. A few are secretly jealous they lack the courage to cut across the field themselves. And the freestarter? She ends up at the pub before anyone else, thus getting the last shepherd's pie of the day, as well as a head start on a pint of ale.

Does that sound too idyllic? That's because I made it up to prove my point! But it's true that freestarters sense unusual alternatives. They respect the decisions of others but feel compelled to live by their own decisions, even if they are unexpected or risky. Because they rarely fit into common molds, freestarters help define and expand reality. Because they seldom have followers, however, freestarters can be perceived as lacking leadership.

So next time you hear a variation of "lead, follow, or

get out of the way," ask yourself what alternatives aren't being mentioned. Not all ways of leading look the same. Traditional leading and following have their place. As we saw earlier, sometimes you do need to get out of the way . . . especially when your business fails. But when none of those are options, don't be afraid to go your own way, even if everyone thinks you're crazy.

SALVAGED FROM SCRIPTURE

What do you call a guy who *sorta* leads and *sorta* follows, but for the most part goes his own way? I call him Noah. Everyone thought he was nuts, but he stands as one of the ultimate go-your-own-way characters in the pages of Scripture.

Noah didn't really try to lead. He just went about the business of listening to and obeying God in an unconventional way—a classic freestarter.[4] Can you imagine the reactions he generated from neighbors? Try building an ark in your front yard and see how people react to you! Not only would your neighbors think you're insane, but the local zoning people would be none too happy about that massive structure in your yard.

Yet Noah really was, somehow, a leader. Not because he had followers. His sum total of followers was his family (who had to follow him) and a bunch of animals (who chose to follow him rather than drown). If you do something everyone thinks is bizarre, and later it turns out you were absolutely

---

[4] He could also be considered a prophet, telling an unpalatable truth to his skeptical neighbors, and he could even be considered an artist if he built an artisanal wooden boat out of reclaimed lumber.

SALVAGED

correct (plus you saved the human race and all the animals), don't you deserve at least a little credit for being a great leader?[5]

The key is that Noah was first and foremost a follower of God. It was his total, action-oriented, frankly illogical commitment to God that made him *just* crazy enough to build an ark and think animals would join him for a sea voyage. He probably *did* care about what others thought, just like we do. He probably *was* hurt by taunts from neighbors and frustrated by unsupportive friends, and spent plenty of sleepless nights wondering if he was indeed crazy. Yet he persevered as a follower of God, simultaneously becoming a leader.

And that's one of the tensions at the heart of all this leadership stuff: The best leaders are, when all is said and done, phenomenal followers.

LESSONS FROM THE JUNKYARD

Don't be afraid to go your own way, even if everyone thinks you're crazy.

The best leaders are, when all is said and done, phenomenal followers.

---

[5] And as happens with a lot of freestarters, the entire experience was so exhausting that he got drunk when the whole thing was over. (See Genesis 9:20-23.)

30
NEVER BUY CHEAP CHAMPAGNE

Lead with your best. Period.

"Hey Roy," you might be asking, "what's the best advice you've ever been given?" (I need at least one of you to ask me that, for the sake of this chapter. Thanks.)

That's a great question—and here's a story that will answer it.

The year was 1981. I was sporting brown hair and a brown mustache. (Have you seen my shiny bald head in the picture on the cover? Then you know why that's amusing.) What you would have been paying attention to, however, was my outfit. I was decked out in my wedding tux, a slate-gray number with charcoal piping, paired with a diagonally striped tie that looked like a UHF channel with bad reception. My wife of two hours, D'Aun, looked lovely in a dress her mother had created.

I can still recall nearly every detail of our wedding reception, which is how I know it was eerily similar to an uncountable number of other receptions.[1] We had rented a historic hotel and restaurant in downtown Pleasanton. There was no live band and very little alcohol. The best man and maid of honor stood for the toasts. We cut the cake but didn't smash it into each other's faces. D'Aun tossed her bouquet to the waiting women. Some of my extended family had deserted the ballroom in favor of the bar. D'Aun's grandfather dropped rice down my back when he hugged me goodbye. And soon we were ready to drive away in Dad's white diesel Cadillac (which broke down two days later).

"Hey Roy," you might be asking, "that's a pretty boring story . . . weren't you going to talk about the best advice you've ever been given?"

Yeah, yeah, I'm getting there. You just needed a bit of background. Anyway, we were getting ready to leave our extremely average, normal, standard, but wonderful wedding reception, when out of the blue my older brother, Geoff, gave me a piece of exceptional and life-changing advice.

I was only twenty-two, but Geoff was thirty-five at the time, with two kids and a mortgage. He was doing the whole middle-of-life thing, while I was bright-eyed and bushy-tailed. Geoff walked toward me across the parquet floor, his

---

[1] Also, our longtime employee Walt, who was like a grandfather to me, had a newfangled video camera, with a battery pack so large and heavy he had to wear it on a belt.

arm extended. I reached out to shake his hand, and as I did so he slipped something into my palm. I could tell it was cash.

"I've only got one bit of advice for you," he said, holding my grip. "Never buy cheap champagne." When he released my hand a small smile briefly touched his face, and then he turned and walked away.

Turns out it was a one-hundred-dollar bill—a big sum for a newlywed making fifteen hundred a month! What surprised me that day about Geoff's advice, and gift, was that he meant it literally. He wanted D'Aun and me to have a wonderful, memorable, story-worthy honeymoon. He actually wanted us to buy a bottle of *real* champagne for one hundred dollars rather than a cheap bottle of "sparkling wine." He didn't want us to parcel out the money on a series of small purchases, and God forbid we put it toward the grocery bill. His gift was generous, funny, and loving, all at the same time.

I know my brother well. Nearly all of the things he loves in life can be categorized by a single word: *good*. Good food, good people, good horses. Good cars, good intentions, and, yes, good champagne.

"Hey Roy," you might be asking, "the story is a *little* better now, but . . . is that all? Is that *seriously* the best advice you've ever received?"

Yes, and here's why. "Never buy cheap champagne" has taken on a far deeper meaning for me over the years.

Some of us make it a habit to save the good things for later. We reserve certain possessions for special occasions, only to look back and notice there was never a moment *quite* special enough. Fine china from our wedding goes in a cabinet, never to see the light of day. An expensive bottle of champagne is never enjoyed.

Now, if we were only talking about plates or drinks, who would care? But deeper, more sacred things can fall victim to the same temptation.

We love our spouses, but we don't take the time or energy to create special moments often enough. We keep our hearts in the cabinet, locked away for a special occasion, but the special occasion never comes. And soon we look back and notice how *cheap* the relationship has become.

We do this with our children. We do this with God. We focus so intently on the required, the practical, the efficient, that we miss the magical. The gloriously wasteful.

We do this with our leadership as well. True leaders give the best of themselves in each situation. No skimping, no saving the "expensive" part of themselves for some future occasion.

You don't need to buy champagne all the time—but when you do, never buy the cheap stuff.

SALVAGED FROM SCRIPTURE

Scripture is full of examples of actions that are gloriously wasteful, but few top the actions of Mary as recorded in John 12. Jesus is the guest of honor at a party, and all the other guests are relaxing at the table, when out of nowhere, Mary breaks open an expensive bottle of perfume and pours it on Jesus' feet.

How expensive? Try thirty thousand bucks, give or take. (Scripture tells us it was a year's wages for a laborer.)

This is a staggering amount of money poured on the feet of a man who would soon be arrested and executed by the state. The disciples are angry, especially the traitor, but Jesus celebrates the action.

Almost as if he's telling his friends—and telling us—to never buy cheap champagne.

LESSONS FROM THE JUNKYARD

Never buy cheap champagne.

We reserve certain possessions for special occasions, only to look back and notice there was never a moment quite *special enough.*

True leaders give the best of themselves in each situation. No skimping, no saving the "expensive" part of themselves for some future occasion.

31
ACTA NON VERBA

Deeds not words.

There is a story about my dad few have heard. It is woven from three of the characteristics that most defined him. First was his fierce love of life. That was a strength that helped him rise from rags to riches and kept him active for years as he battled Parkinson's disease. Second was his fierce streak of personal independence. And third was the time he spent at Kings Point Merchant Marine Academy,[1] where he was drilled in the concept of service above self, and where he took to heart the motto *Acta Non Verba*.

---

[1] Dad joined the merchant marine, which is a civilian fleet of ships that becomes attached to the navy during wartime, because he didn't want to kill anyone. Nearly ten thousand brave mariners died in World War II, and at a higher rate—almost one in twenty-five—than any other branch of the armed services. For more information on this topic, see http://www.usmm.org/faq.html.

Action not talk. Deeds not words. That was my father's motto too . . . and if those elements of his personality got him in hot water at times, they were also his greatest strengths.

This story is seldom told because it is almost too much to tell. It isn't funny or flippant, but it is one unforgettable leadership lesson. I was young when this happened and didn't fully understand it at the time, but I've never stopped thinking about it.

It's 1969 or 1970, and we're driving a country highway, somewhere near my older brother Geoff's house in New Mexico. We've picked up Geoff and his wife, Nancy, and now the five of us—Geoff, Nancy, Mom, Dad, and me—are headed somewhere that I've long since forgotten. The road is winding along the side of a mountain, with a drop of a few hundred feet on one side and a steep cliff on the other. We pass occasional stray rocks that have fallen and clutter the side of the road.

We round a sharp corner, and there's a car dangling over the edge of the roadway, just like in a movie. The front wheels are over the edge, and it looks like the car could go over at any moment. Three seconds later, we skid to a stop behind the car, and Dad jumps out. Geoff jumps out.

Mom spins toward the back seat, arm out. "Don't you get out, Roy! You stay right—"

I jump out anyway. I see Dad at the driver's door. I see Geoff lugging a large rock and wedging it behind one of the woman's rear tires. I copy my brother, sprinting for a nearby rock and carrying it back to the car. I hear the woman driver through her open window, sobbing, sobbing, and I can see Dad's lips moving. His hands are out, palms down, like he's trying to calm her.

Mom and Nancy are at the side of the road now, waving their arms. I know they're flagging down someone willing to race to the closest pay phone to call for help.

Geoff and I add another two rocks, and another two. We wedge them in as tight as we can because every few seconds the car lurches, like the driver has her foot on the brake and the accelerator at the same time.

The tires are as secure as we're going to make them, and we stop to breathe. I glance at Geoff as the woman revs the engine again. We both know: She's trying to kill herself.

I sidle slightly closer to Dad, despite the terror in my chest. I hear him talking. Calm and low, but firm, like I've heard him talk to a horse before. He's telling the woman everything he's about to do, step-by-step, and when I hear it my chest gets even tighter.

His actions match every word. The next few seconds feel like years as we watch. He touches the door, takes the handle, opens the door, gently talking all the while. He puts one hand on the steering wheel, and then—*don't, Dad, don't*—he eases in so his right hip is on the seat and his right leg is inside the car. He's not asking the woman, he's telling. He presses down on the brake pedal with his right foot, he uses his left foot to set the emergency brake, he reaches over with his right hand and shifts the transmission into park.

The woman's head is in her hands and she's sobbing louder than ever and then she just . . . goes limp. She gives up.

Dad turns off the ignition and takes out the keys, and then his body relaxes too. He's not saying anything now. He's just sitting close to the woman, close enough for her to slump against him, sobbing, terrified, confused.

I shudder. I walk to my mother, and she puts her arm around me. No one speaks. A few minutes go by, and a car passes. A bird calls high above. A few more minutes pass. Dad hasn't moved and neither has the woman.

Sirens approach. Dad glances over as the police car stops on the shoulder. He turns back to the woman, smiles at her, and steps away from the car. He's holding the keys.

The officer steps to the driver's door. "License and registration, please."

Dad is getting ready to hand the keys over, but when he hears the officer, his arm freezes. He fixes the officer with a stare that makes him take a half step back. It's the stare of a man who grew up poor, who hustled pickles and chocolate cake out of parties so he could eat, who saw death and destruction as he fought for his country in a world war, who pulled greasy parts out of wrecked cars so he could support his family, who stared down drug addicts and Hells Angels alike. It's a stare that conveys disgust, anger, and fearlessness. It's also a stare of desperation, of a man who has just risked his life for a stranger without thinking twice. Then Dad shakes his head, hands over the keys, and strides back to our car.

We get back in our car. I face the front and see Dad's hands shaking a bit on the wheel. Mom is crying silently. My brother and sister-in-law are sitting still beside me, breathing deep.

We pull away. I look back and see the police officer talking to the woman, see the rocks we wedged under her rear wheels. See everything growing smaller.

And then we turn the corner.

———————

To this day, I can taste that fear. I can hear the woman's engine revving, hear the tires lurching against the dirt and the rocks.

And to this day, I believe that event was a beautiful summation of what defined my father. Caring, loving, compassionate, and desperate to see life continue, even in the midst of self-hatred. Especially in the midst of self-hatred.

The only way he could do that was to act.

No planning. No deliberation. He simply sprang from the car and figured things out as he went along. I believe that's why the policeman's manner infuriated my father. Having acted without regard for his own safety, Dad became disgusted by the insistence on procedural routine. The officer missed the main point: There was a desperate woman who needed help.

That was the *only* point my father had seen.

Dad was a special man. I knew that as a kid. I know it even better now that he is gone.

SALVAGED FROM SCRIPTURE

After a story like that, well, where can we go from here? Scripture is *filled* with stories we could use. But after consulting with my publisher, the decision has been made *not* to include the entire book of James.

We've also decided not to include Isaiah 1:16-17 (or hundreds of other verses from that book).

Or the Sermon on the Mount. Or Matthew 25:34-46.

Or Hosea 6.

Or Amos 5:21-24.

In fact, now that I've wasted all this time with preamble, I only have space for three more sentences.

Read everything I just mentioned. But if you can't find the time for that, here's the condensed version.

I will show you my faith by my deeds.

JAMES 2:18

LESSON FROM THE JUNKYARD

"I will show you my faith by my deeds" (James 2:18).

CONCLUSION

A veteran leader I know was recently presented with a commissioned oil painting. This leader is a college president, scholar, and writer who has a deep admiration for Saint Augustine, the famed theologian and leader of the fourth-century church. Saint Augustine—who basically invented the genre of writing-about-yourself, for which I am grateful—managed to profoundly influence his contemporaries *and* world culture, philosophy, and religion for the next sixteen hundred years. So he's kind of a big deal.

Anyway, the painting shows Saint Augustine kneeling at the foot of the cross, looking at the feet of Jesus. (If you're wondering how someone born more than three centuries after the death of Jesus could possibly be at the Crucifixion, lighten up—it's art!) Augustine is portrayed as a bearded penitent, staring through the years and across several countries at the source of his life's work and faith. He kneels in humility, focused on the feet of Jesus.

Focused on the feet.

There is something both beautiful and profound in that. In the presence of the greatest leader in history, Augustine focuses on . . . the feet.

Those were the feet that took Jesus *into* the world, filled with goodness and motivated by love. Jesus didn't come to sit in his office and write books—he came to *act*. His feet carried him from Galilee to Samaria to Judea, and eventually to Jerusalem. And ultimately, they carried him—and his cross—to the place of his execution.

Saint Augustine was a leader of leaders, the bishop of Hippo and a giant of the early church. And when I look at Saint Augustine in this painting, I follow his gaze to the feet of Jesus.

I am drawn to Christ.

A true leader is one who, when followed, draws people to Christ. Too often, we are drawn merely to the leader, however, and not to Christ. Too often, the leader's eyes are focused on things other than Christ.

There is a tension here that runs throughout this book: Sometimes we as Christian leaders *do* need to focus on things other than Christ. Like finalizing a project with a fast-approaching deadline. If the website needs to go live in three days, we don't have a ton of time to pray and journal, right?

Too often, however, we neglect to return our attention to Christ.

When that happens—when we become habituated to leading without Christ—we harm ourselves, our employees, and our organizations.

There is a natural movement in leadership, a balance between humility and confidence. Between patience and productivity, wisdom and risk, faith and caution. The more we follow Christ, the more we will be drawn to the right things for the right reasons and the more we will navigate the tension and keep things in balance. When leaders are willing to approach the feet of Christ and kneel, those same leaders will know when it is time to *leave* the cross and go into the world, for the sake of the world.

Look, I wish I was a perfect leader. I'm not, obviously. I wish I could tell you exactly what to do at exactly the right time in exactly the right way. But I can't, and no self-described leadership expert can.[1]

But I can ask you, and myself, this absolutely foundational question: If you consider yourself a leader, are you pointing people toward Christ?

No matter what type of leader you are—business, ministry, artist, prophet, freestarter, education, government, entertainment—when all is said and done, are you keeping your gaze on the feet of Jesus? And do those who follow you want to follow that gaze?

If you've read the book to this point, then it's clear you wish to be exactly that kind of leader. So now you should begin.

---

[1] Seriously. No one can . . . so if someone tries to, you can safely ignore it!

ACKNOWLEDGMENTS

It's a Thursday evening when D'Aun asks, "Want to invite someone over for a glass of wine this weekend?"

"Sure," I answer. "How about a few of the people who helped
with the book?"

"Isn't that a pretty long list? Who did you have in mind?"

The people who have taught me about leadership flash through
my memory, from wrecking yards to construction crews, from brokers to pastors. Many modeled a certain grittiness in their leadership that changed me, mostly for the better. We could invite them,
but most won't come, and some might not even remember me.

Thinking it best to start with the obvious, I answer with "Well,
you, of course."

"Well, *thank you*," she quips.

"And Rachel and Jedd, of course," I continue, ignoring her
sarcasm. "Also Anne Stoneberger for all the work on the edits, plus
David Zimmerman and the NavPress team. Tawny Johnson was a
great agent and should get an invite."

"What about David?"

"Oh, duh—yeah, David Jacobsen, of course. He did all the
heavy lifting. And he might be the only person who writes even

snarkier than I do. Oh, and Nancy Ortberg. Remember when she originally had the idea for this book? That was at least ten, maybe fifteen years ago. And of course, my old buddy Bob Goff, since he was nice enough to write the foreword."

"Good. Sounds like a fun group of people."

"Yeah, but . . . would you mind if I invite a few more?"

D'Aun looks at me warily. "Who else?"

I clear my throat, a little concerned about her reaction, then quickly jabber, "It would just be a few of the people who taught me something about leadership or gave good feedback on the book. Roger Dermody, Mark Parcher, Adrienne Parcher, Greg Lundell, Jen Hollingsworth, Brenda Salter McNeil, Nick Parisi, Ken Wytsma, Debbie Hall, Gayle Beebe, Carol Houston, Stan Gaede, Verne Sharma, Tony Campolo, Charlie Brown, Jody Vanderwel, Steve Madsen, Bishop Wright, Mark Roberts, Jacquelline Fuller, Mark Zoradi, my brother Geoff, my mom, of course—"

"Okay, stop!" she interrupts. "I get it. This started as inviting a few friends over, but you want a big party."

I pause, reflecting on her words, thinking of all the people who helped me as a leader and helped with this book. It's a long list, scattered across the globe, sprinkled through the decades, and some I never met. Sadly, a few are now gone from this world: Max De Pree, Peter Drucker, Dallas Willard, Jane Higa, Clarence Sands, Andy Grove. My dad is especially missed.

"You know, I truly am thankful for all those who helped," I say a few minutes later. "But to paraphrase Johnny Cash, I think I just want this evening, a bottle of wine, and you."

"Sounds great," she says, smiling.

And it is.